In today's play-it-safe culture, this is a must-read book for anyone who wants to take smarter risks that elevate themselves and others to higher ground. If fear of failing or falling short has ever held you back, this book is for you. Buy it. Read it. Take the leap!

— MARSHALL GOLDSMITH, THINKERS50 WORLD #1 EXECUTIVE
COACH & LEADERSHIP THINKER

Creating a better world requires courage. Stop Playing Safe *gives you a roadmap to take the bold action required to move ahead in a world where uncertainty and acceleration are equal realities. If you're looking for an inspired step forward in leadership and life this book is a must read!*

— MAYA HARI, VICE PRESIDENT, GLOBAL STRATEGY AND OPERATIONS, TWITTER

Margie is a true expert on the science of success. Her new book is both inspiring and practical. It's a powerful manual for creating the life of your dreams.

— SIIMON REYNOLDS, BEST-SELLING AUTHOR OF *WHY PEOPLE FAIL*

Margie Warrell provides powerful and practical advice for overcoming our innate fear of risk and vulnerability. It bears reading and re-reading for all who strive to become their best selves.

— DR GORDON LIVINGSTON, AUTHOR OF *TOO SOON OLD, TOO LATE SMART*

Adapting to change and taking chances are critical to your success. This book will help you with both. Get it, read it, enjoy the results.

— JON GORDON, BEST-SELLING AUTHOR OF
THE ENERGY BUS AND *THE SEED*

Stop Playing Safe *provides a roadmap to navigate uncertainty and find the courage to create meaningful changes in your workplace, career and life.*

— REBECCA HEINO, PROFESSOR OF MANAGEMENT,
MCDONOUGH SCHOOL OF BUSINESS, GEORGETOWN UNIVERSITY

T0044915

One look at the title of my last book, and then this one, should tell you why I like it! Stop Playing Safe *will help you harness the courage to take the risks that make sense — and give you the success you want.*

Stop Playing Safe *is more than a book; it's a reference guide for living a full and courageous life. It's one of those rare books that is at once original, inspirational and above all, useful. Margie Warrell is a leading voice in the courage building movement and* Stop Playing Safe *proves that too much safety can be a dangerous thing.*

Practical, powerful and inspiring. In uncertain times, it's a guidebook you absolutely must read as it spells out exactly how to handle your challenges and find the confidence to speak up and get ahead in the new economy. Everyone in your company should read it!

It's the risks we don't take that we regret the most. Stop Playing Safe *will give you the courage to do more, experience more, and regret less. Read it. Apply it. Reap the rewards of a braver life.*

STOP PLAYING SAFE

STOP PLAYING SAFE

DR. MARGIE WARRELL

FULLY REVISED **SECOND EDITION**

HOW TO BE **BRAVER** IN YOUR **WORK**, **LEADERSHIP** AND **LIFE**

WILEY

First published in 2021 by John Wiley & Sons Australia, Ltd

42 McDougall St, Milton Qld 4064
Office also in Melbourne

Typeset in Adobe Caslon Pro 11pt/14.5pt

© John Wiley & Sons Australia, Ltd 2021

The moral rights of the author have been asserted

ISBN: 978-0-730-39458-7

NATIONAL
LIBRARY
OF AUSTRALIA

A catalogue record for this
book is available from the
National Library of Australia

Cover design by Wiley
Cover author photo: Lisa Sheldon Photography
Internal author photo: Alise Black

Disclaimer
The material in this publication is of the nature of general comment only, and does not represent professional advice. It is not intended to provide specific guidance for particular circumstances and it should not be relied on as the basis for any decision to take action or not take action on any matter which it covers. Readers should obtain professional advice where appropriate, before making any such decision. To the maximum extent permitted by law, the author and publisher disclaim all responsibility and liability to any person, arising directly or indirectly from any person taking or not taking action based on the information in this publication.

CONTENTS

PART III

TAKE COURAGE SET YOURSELF UP FOR SUCCESS!

ABOUT MARGIE

Dr Margie Warrell brings her diverse international experience in business, coaching and psychology — coupled with a deep passion for unlocking the potential that fear often holds hostage — to inspire braver action in today's increasingly cautious world.

Margie has walked her talk since her childhood growing up in a big family on a small farm in rural Australia. She has lived and worked around the world for more than 25 years, trusted by global brands such as Amazon, Dell, Google, Johnson & Johnson, L'Oreal, Morgan Stanley, NASA and Salesforce to deliver transformative programs that accelerate growth, improve outcomes and strengthen leadership.

A Senior Partner with Korn Ferry's CEO & Leadership advisory practice, Margie is a passionate advocate for inclusive leadership and advancing more women to decision making tables. Named a Top Voice by LinkedIn, Margie is a member of the board of Forbes School of Business & Technology, she regularly shares her expertise in leading media such as CNN, Bloomberg and *The Wall Street Journal*. Margie also shares insights from her conversations with global leaders and luminaries such as Richard Branson, Steve Forbes, Tony Robbins, Bill Marriott, Dr Phil McGraw, Marianne Williamson and Dr John Demartini in her 'Courage Work' *Forbes* column and *Live Brave* podcast.

The titles of Margie's *Live Brave* podcast and other best-selling books — *Find Your Courage, Make Your Mark, Train the Brave* and *You've Got This!* — reflect the passion she brings to her own leadership and life. Margie also loves adventure travel, especially long hikes in beautiful places — from climbing Kilimanjaro with her husband and their four brave-hearted children to exploring national parks near her home outside Washington, DC.

A sought after keynote speaker, Margie regularly shares her insights on living and leading more bravely on social media. She'd love to connect with you there and invites you to sign up for her Live Bravely newsletter at www.margiewarrell.com.

PREFACE

The first edition of this book was written nearly a decade ago, during my first year living back in Australia after over a decade in the USA. At the time, many people were still regaining their footing in the wake of the 2008 global financial crisis which had shaken their sense of security. As fear ran high, I drew on the insights of leaders I'd worked with, as well as my own research, to help people 'rethink risk' and move boldly forward amid the uncertainty.

This revised second edition has been written after another global move — this time from Singapore back to the USA — and another, even greater, global crisis. I think it's fair to say the COVID-19 pandemic jolted our sense of security and raised the 'fear factor' to whole new levels.

As I witnessed people making irrational decisions driven solely by fear (one person I knew cashed in their entire retirement savings, fearing Armageddon was nigh), I felt compelled to update this book and streamline it.

Of course, there will always be legitimate reasons for going with the safest option. Yet when uncertainty looms large, we must be all the more vigilant to discern between the fears that are serving us and those that are driving us to make overly cautious decisions in our work, in how we live and how we lead. Because while playing it too safe can provide a short-term sense of security, it ultimately keeps us from taking the very actions that would help us become more secure — individually and collectively — over the longer term.

While the world may *feel* like a riskier place today, the truth is that there have always been risks. The difference is that in today's digital 24/7 world, we're now continually bombarded with information that makes life appear riskier. Only when we dare to 'lean towards risk' and venture onto new ground can we seize the opportunities hidden within our challenges, turning our setbacks into stepping stones, and leading ourselves and others to higher ground and a more, not less, secure world.

So if the title of this book spoke to you, it wasn't by chance. I hope the pages that follow will embolden you to embrace uncertainty and take the risks required to open up new possibilities for you and those around you.

In today's culture of fear, daring to rise above our instinctual desire to play it safe, to take brave action amid the risks, has become ever more imperative.

INTRODUCTION

Please indulge me for just one moment with a little game of 'make believe'.

Imagine stepping into the shoes of your 'future self', ten years from now, looking back on you today, reading this, facing an unknown future but eager to make the most of it.

What would you love to have experienced in your work and career, and in your life outside it? What impact would you love to have made on the lives of others? What skills or mastery would you like to have gained? What kind of person would you like to have become?

Ten years may feel like a long time away right now. Yet you thought that ten years ago and look … here you are.

So the next ten years is going to pass for you one way or another. The question is, what will you do with it?

Life is the lump sum of our choices. Too often, though, our choices are driven by fear — fear of what might go wrong; fear of not having what it takes; fear of making a fool of ourselves, 'found out' as unworthy or inadequate in some way. Often, we're not even aware of how fear is pulling the invisible strings of our daily decisions but if you're not waking up inspired by your future, then it most certainly is.

We live in a culture of fear, so it's little wonder that despite people living longer today than at any point in history — indicating fewer (not more!) threats to our survival — millions of people today spend their lives living in the shadow of fear, continually avoiding what scares them rather than pursuing what inspires them.

The term VUCA was coined to describe the volatile, uncertain, complex and ambiguous nature of modern life. But let's be honest here — we've never had certainty! However, in our overwired lives today, our news streams bombard us with reasons to bite our nails, stock up on toilet paper and play it safe. Fear has become normalised to the point that we cannot even recognise how many decisions are driven by it.

Yet time and time again history has shown that when fear runs most rampant, brave action reaps the greatest rewards. It's why we must be deliberate not to let fear sit in the driver's seat of our lives. We must commit to being braver — in how we work, live and lead.

Countless times in my own life, from my relatively confined childhood on a small dairy farm in rural Australia to my adult life living around the world from Papua New Guinea to Singapore, I have found that each time I decide to take action in the presence of my fear — to *not* play life safe — I dilute the power fear holds over me and amplify my own.

The world has weathered one heck of a storm since the first edition of this book. Before the COVID-19 pandemic I used to write about how afraid some people were of killer viruses and how unlikely a pandemic actually is. Well … the unlikely event happened and most of us were caught off guard anyway. It triggered a cascading crisis that dialled up the fear factor in our homes and communities, in our schools and organisations, and at decision-making tables the world over.

> **Left unchecked, fear can narrow our thinking, derail our decision-making and keep us from seeing, much less seizing, the opportunities that always exist amid disruption, although often out of plain sight. It can also drive us to over-estimate the risks, making us suffer more from our fear than from the source of it.**

It's why, in this VUCA world we inhabit, the thinking and behaviours that got you to where you are today will be insufficient to take you to where you want to be ten years from now. As the world has changed, so too must you change how you engage in it.

I have written this book because I hold a deep and unwavering belief in our potential as 'human becomings' to create lives rich in meaning and to move all humanity to higher ground. Yet in my work that spans many countries, cultures and continents, I constantly encounter people trapped inside prisons of their own making, hemmed in by the borders of their own imagination, living under the long shadow of fear.

The truth is that you have all the resources within you to create a deeply meaningful and rewarding life, regardless of what you've done (or failed to do) before, or what is going on in your life right now. However, if you sometimes wonder otherwise, you're not alone. Global employee surveys tell us that millions of people think that what they do each day doesn't matter and that they are powerless to change their environment. The cost to the commercial bottom line is in the billions. The cost to the human spirit is immeasurable. Underlying this disengagement is fear in many guises — of failure, success, rejection, exposure, not having enough ... of not *being* enough.

Countless business books are filled with strategies for becoming a more proficient networker, strategist, salesperson, negotiator, 'hi-po' employee and leader. Very few address the deep-seated fears and complex interplay of unconscious cognitive biases that form the human condition, and that keep us from applying them.

While this book is written for you, the individual, it will benefit any team, enterprise or organisation. After all, organisations are made up of people. As such, people are their number one resource and the fear that stifles their potential — their creativity, collaboration and collective ingenuity — is their number one threat. No organisation can compete in today's world unless those who are part of it feel emboldened to 'push the envelope' of possibility. This entails risk and demands courage.

This book comprises eight chapters, divided into three parts.

Part I: *Core Courage* (chapters 1 to 3) forms the foundation for all good decision making and forward-leaning action.

Part II: *Working Courage* (chapters 4 to 7) provides concepts and practical strategies to be more courageous and effective in handling the challenges and seizing the opportunities in your work and life.

Part III: *Take Courage* (chapter 8) is where the rubber hits the road as you make the changes that prompted you to pick up this book in the first place. Part III will set you up for success, creating an environment that emboldens you to take smarter risks and pave new pathways toward your biggest future and a better world.

Back in 2019, none of us could have imagined in our wildest dreams that in 2020 the world would be knocked off its axis with the cascading crisis of the COVID-19 pandemic. Yet in the midst of having to deal with challenges we never expected, much less planned for, many people discovered within themselves more courage, tenacity and resilience than they knew they had.

None of us can know what challenges the years ahead will bring. The world is changing so fast, it's hard to imagine what it will look like two years from now, much less 20. All of which begs the question: what mindset will you adopt to navigate the uncertainty ahead? Because in the end what matters far less than the challenges you face is the mindset you bring to them.

As uncertain as this time in human history is, one thing remains certain: only those who are willing to fling their arms wide to the full spectrum of human experience will be able to seize the opportunities that surround each of us every single day. In the end, there is no success without the possibility of failure. As Helen Keller said, 'Life is either a daring adventure or nothing at all.'

PART I
CORE COURAGE

BUILD YOUR FOUNDATION

Courage is the price that life exacts for granting peace.

AMELIA EARHART

1

KNOW YOUR WHY

Decide how you will measure success

If we do not believe within ourselves this deeply rooted feeling that there is something higher than ourselves, we shall never find the strength to evolve into something higher.

RUDOLF STEINER

You've read the stories. Of the accidental hero diving into a frozen river or lifting a car many times their body weight to rescue a total stranger. Of the desperate mother walking hundreds of miles under the blistering sun to seek help for her child.

In the face of impossible odds, people have tapped into reserves of seeming superhuman power, unlocking strength, courage and steel-like determination that would otherwise have lain dormant. And often not just for their own sake, but for the sake of someone else. Sometimes even a complete stranger.

Perhaps you've experienced such a moment in your own life where you've tapped into a deeper source of power and courage within you; perhaps that almost surprised you. Maybe you found yourself in your own 'impossible' predicament, but resolved that nothing was going to stop you.

A personal crisis. A 'must achieve' goal. A 'mission impossible' you just had to pull off.

Your task was compelling. Your focus lasered. Your potential ignited.

Purpose does that. It's like the energy of light focused through a magnifying glass. While diffused, unfocused light has little use and less power, when its energy is concentrated — as through a magnifying glass — that same light can set fire to paper.

Focus its energy even more, as with a laser beam, and its power is magnified enough to cut through steel.

> **A clear and compelling sense of purpose enables you to harness the resources within you to cut through the barriers around you and accomplish the extraordinary. Purpose focuses your energy — physical, intellectual, emotional and spiritual — towards an end goal that compels you out of your comfort zone and pushes you forward regardless of the obstacles.**

Of course, few people feel that burning fire in their belly every day of their lives. But it is imperative to connect to what ignites that inner spark within us if we want to take our lives to the next level and forge a more rewarding future than what we might otherwise be on track to do.

Given we are wealthier today than at any point in human history, there is clearly a marked difference between 'well off' and 'wellbeing'. Unlike animals, which are driven simply to survive, we humans crave more from life than mere survival. Without an answer to the question 'Survival for the sake of what?', we can quickly fall into disillusionment and distraction and spend our precious years living with a lingering sense of despair. Adam Grant described this state of languishing as 'the neglected middle child of mental health' — the void between depression and flourishing. The kind of living that isn't fully living.

The alarming increase in rates of substance abuse, depression and suicide, along with the growing reliance on antidepressant medications, seems to indicate many are doing just that. Employee engagement statistics point to a crisis of purpose on an unprecedented scale.

FOR THE SAKE OF WHAT?

You are capable of achieving inspiring things and living a deeply rewarding life that lights you up and elevates all around you. Yet the instinctive desire for safety — wired into the back recesses of your brain from our hunter-gatherer days — will always pull hard against, well, your desire for pretty much anything else. Let's face it, it's far easier to stick on your current path than to put yourself 'out there' and risk making a royal fool of yourself — at least in the short term.

Our brains are hard-wired to avoid risk. We have an inbuilt antenna on constant alert for potential threats that might disrupt our status quo (even if it's a miserable status quo). It's why we're still here and many species that roamed the African plains 100 000 years ago are not. But we're not just talking physical safety. We're talking emotional safety too. Embedded into our psychological DNA is a deep, instinctive desire to avoid social rejection or humiliation and steer well clear of situations that might dint our pride or wound our ego. Our ego is as thirsty as it is fragile.

It's why so many people spend so much of their lives *not* taking the very actions that would change what they don't like about their lives. Why they stay in jobs they hate or in relationships that leave them lonely. It's also why people in leadership roles often make over-cautious decisions and instead act to shore up their power and protect their pride. I'm sure you've witnessed this as often as I have.

It's also why, before we move any further into this book, it's important for you to identify what you care about more than protecting your ego or your short-term comfort. If you can't do that, you'll never risk it.

For the sake of what will you be brave?

That is, why should you bother pursuing challenges that stretch you? Why stick your neck out, have that brave conversation or make that big ask? Why risk losing the comfortable familiarity of your life right now?

To answer this question, you need to reflect not just on what you want in your career–business–life, but who you want to become by what you do each day.

> In today's superficial selfie culture, where so many get sucked into a daily wrestling match with their fear of being left out or left behind, connecting to a deeper purpose that transcends the trivial and temporary has become 'mission critical'. Only when we connect to a cause that transcends our ego's need for status can we evolve to something higher.

THE PURPOSE OF LIFE IS A LIFE OF PURPOSE — WHAT DO YOU WANT YOUR LIFE TO STAND FOR?

Psychiatrist Viktor Frankl, the only member of his family to survive the Nazi concentration camps, devoted his life to understanding man's need for meaning and the power of purpose.

Frankl bore witness not only to the murder of his extended family, but to the death of thousands of men who were unable to survive the barbaric conditions in which they found themselves. However, he also saw men whose resolve to live enabled them to fight off despair, defy death and survive long enough to bear witness to the brutality and deprivation forced upon them.

His experiences in World War II and thereafter led him to believe that the power of the human spirit can only be fully unleashed when our purpose for living transcends merely surviving.

A clear sense of purpose enables you to focus your efforts away from distracted busyness and zero-calorie, self-absorbed activities that do not feed the soul, towards those activities that do. Nowhere is this more important than in how you employ your skills, talents and time throughout your work, and indeed your life.

THE SEARCH FOR MEANING LIES AT THE HEART OF A MEANINGFUL LIFE

You have everything — yes, *everything* — it takes to achieve whole new levels of fulfilment in your work and to positively impact the lives of everyone around you, directly and indirectly. But doing so will require you to make a deep commitment to refuse to give in to the myriad fear-laden forces that pull so many clever, creative and capable people into the crowded ranks of mediocrity.

It's conditional on you daring to take a risk — to lay your pride and vulnerability on the line for the sake of a nobler cause. To make your own personal pledge not to let fear hold the reins in your aspirations, in your conversations and in your daily actions.

> What you *don't* have right now — position, power, status, skills — pales in comparison to all that you *do* have. Stand tall in your worth and embrace your one-of-a-kind brand of brilliance. There are things that will never be done if you do not do them. So if not now, then when? And if not you, then who? Your journey to this point in time has landed you in the perfect place to make the difference your difference makes.

Back in the 1960s Viktor Frankl said that ever more today people have the means to live but not the meaning to live for. The trendline has not improved. Studies have found that once we earn enough to have our basic needs fulfilled, extra money adds only incrementally to our happiness. What a tragedy it is that so many people spend so much of their lives desperate to be doing something other than what they are doing.

Little wonder that a study in the *Harvard Business Review* reported that more than 90 per cent of employees would be willing to trade a percentage of their lifetime earnings for greater meaning in their work. When asked for the specifics, 2000+ respondents — workers across all ages and salary groups — said that they would forgo an average of 23 per cent of their future lifetime earnings in order to secure a meaningful job until they retire.

> We all need a 'reason for being' that transcends the superficial, that taps into the deep human yearning to leave the world a little better off for our time here; to have lived a life that mattered even if our name was never put in lights and our story never etched in history.

As a boy, my dad spent several years living in a corrugated-iron shed at the water's edge along the south-east coastline of Australia. (It's a pretty but little-known place, without even its own postcode, called Nungurner, if you care to look it up.) Dad fondly recalls those years, living barefoot and subsisting off the land and lake, among the happiest of his life. Every day my 'nana' would cook the fish they caught in a camp oven on the sand beside their shed. Every night, they slept in the rafters since, when the tide came in, their sand floor became the lake.

When Dad was 13 his parents bought a small dairy farm and a few years later, at 16, he left school to work on it. He spent most of the next 50 years milking cows — every morning and evening — and only just making ends meet and raising his seven kids (I'm number two). A man of deep faith, Dad often prayed to God to help him find if there was a deeper purpose to his life beyond being a humble 'dairy cocky' as he called himself. He said it was not until his 50s that he realised he'd been living his purpose all along — being a loving husband and father, and a generous member of his local church and rural community.

Now well in his 80s, Dad is back living by the water's edge just a few steps from the 'red shed' he lived in as a boy. Whenever I visit my parents, it's near guaranteed that Dad will tell me at some point during my stay — often over one of the many pots of tea we share or out fishing in his old boat — that he feels like the richest man in all the world. While Dad is far from wealthy in a material sense, his gratitude and love for his life and family connect him to a more meaningful sense of wealth than money alone can ever buy.

Given most of us live with creature comforts that our parents, much less grandparents, could not have imagined, the answer to a more rewarding life cannot be found by chasing more money, but by finding greater meaning. As Lynne Twist, author of *The Soul of Money*, shared on my *Live Brave* podcast: 'Living from a space that more is better just leaves us on a chase with no end and a race without a winner.' If we think that money is the answer to meaning, then even too much is never enough. After all, there'll always be someone with a bigger yacht.

Finding your 'reason for being' takes deep reflection and serious soul searching — something many of us are masters at avoiding. As John W Gardner, who ran Carnegie Corporation for many years, once said, 'Human beings have always employed an enormous variety of clever devices for running away from themselves.'

In the hurly-burly of life, we run the risk of missing out on life itself. It's why gifting yourself with time out to become truly present to this finite and fragile gift we call life, what you want to do with it, and why that matters at a soul-deep level, is an investment that pays life's richest dividends. Only once you connect to a purpose that eclipses your fear can you summon the courage to honour your gifts and heed the siren call of your spirit.

This may sound deep, but I didn't write this book to help you live a more successful, shallow life. That said, I also didn't write it to convince you to change career, quit your job or start a side hustle (though perhaps you will). Rather, I wrote it to help you get clear about what you want to *do*, who you want to *be* and *what* brave actions you must take to live your highest purpose; to do more of what lights you up and less of what doesn't. And on the days when life feels like a grind — as it did many times for my dad getting up before dawn each morning, or enduring long droughts with little income — to press on in the sure knowledge that it's not *what we get* by living our lives in ways that honour our deepest values and noblest intentions, but it is *who we become* in the process.

The philosopher Friedrich Nietzsche once said, 'He who has a why can endure any how.' A quick web search will yield hundreds of methods for discovering your why; your 'reason for being'. But let's face it, neither an app nor a guru can give you the answers that reside within you. That said, the right questions can help you uncover your why. And there are compelling reasons why you must.

> President Kennedy once wrote that 'Effort and courage are not enough without purpose and direction'. In fact, effort and courage can land you in all sorts of trouble if not anchored to core values, principles and purpose.

Living and leading from *why* provides a compass for navigating your life. As shown in figure 1, only when you are clear about *why* what you do matters can you muster the courage to be *who* you must be to figure out *what* needs to be done to achieve what you want and change what you don't. Only then can you *have* what you yearn for most in life. Which, at the deepest level, is peace.

Figure 1: begin with *why*

Now indulge me for a moment and just lay aside any doubts or cynicism on your mental bookshelf for a moment. In the space that opens up, give yourself permission to sit with the possibility that there are things that you — and *only* you — can do that will never be done if you don't do them (or at least not in the same way you would). Consider for a moment that it's not been a lack of opportunity that's held you back but a lack of clarity about what you truly want your life to stand for. *Until now.*

The truth is that most of us humans live in a restricted circle of our full potential. Even using conservative estimates, neurobiologists estimate that the human brain has approximately 100 trillion neuron junctions which, in layman language, means that our possible mental states exceed the total number of atoms in the universe. That's a lot of potential left under the bed.

Unleashing it requires focusing your inner 'laser beam' with a reason to set your alarm before sunrise (except if you live in Alaska), roll up your sleeves, and take a brave leap of faith in the moments it matters most. There will be many. Only then will you be able to resist succumbing to pride's ever-tempting pull that confines so many to lives of immaculate mediocrity. Only then will you build your 'courage muscles' for the bigger, albeit sometimes messy, life you have it within you to live.

HOW DO YOU WANT TO MEASURE YOUR LIFE?

The multiple crises of the COVID-19 pandemic jolted most of us out of our comfort zone, shaking up our lives in ways we could never have predicted, much less planned for. Yet when the world you know falls apart and you're compelled to piece it back together in a whole new way, it can pull back the curtain on what truly matters to you.

> If you are not feeling 'on fire' in your life (or are bona fide languishing), then step back from your busy *doing* to re-evaluate who you are *being* in the storybook of your own life. As you do, ask yourself: is this a story you'd want to read one day? Is how you're showing up for life aligned with how you want to measure your life?

About a year after we got married, my husband Andrew and I decided to pursue our shared vision of living and working internationally. At the time we were both working for multinational organisations in Melbourne, Australia. Over a bottle of wine one evening we came up with a playful competition: who could land us the first overseas assignment.

We had images of us enjoying the high life as a young married couple in New York, London, Paris, or maybe somewhere more exotic … Shanghai, Hong Kong, Rome … Berlin, maybe?

A few months later Andrew arrived home one evening excited but also a little nervous. He thought he'd landed us an opportunity … 'But it's not where we were thinking,' he said with some apprehension.

My mind started racing. Rio? Mexico City? Delhi? Kuala Lumpur?

Nope. Port Moresby.

Papua New Guinea. Mecca for cultural anthropologists since some of PNG's 600 indigenous tribes (speaking 850 languages!) had only just encountered modern civilisation.

Truth was, Port Moresby, the not-very-sophisticated capital of PNG, wasn't on my top 500 list. But we were ready for adventure and, not wanting to spend our lives in the one city (or country), we signed up.

While many people thought we were crazy — at the time it was one of the most dangerous countries in the world outside a war zone — we saw it as an adventure.

So off we went and I traded my 'upwardly mobile' career at a top consulting firm to work for a small PNG-based marketing company. It was an interesting role and I found myself doing everything from directing television commercials to running market research for global brands selling everything from beer to instant noodles.

It would be easy to fill a book with intrepid tales from our time in PNG, which still had remote tribes practising cannibalism at the time. But while it was filled with some off-the-beaten-track adventures (like climbing Mount Wilhelm, the tallest peak in Oceania at 4509 metres) and scary moments (like evacuating political coups amid tear gas and being held up at gunpoint), one of the most profound experiences I had was discovering my gift for helping others to, in the simplest language, 'get out of their own way' and be braver.

Yet while 'helping people be braver' was very rewarding, I had a limited 'toolbox' beyond my own hard-won wisdom, so I returned to study, enrolling in distance postgrad studies in Psychology. At the time, I'd never heard of coaching. I didn't even know there were people who spoke on stages and were paid for it. I just knew that helping people uncover their fears and take more courageous action was something that lit me up and came naturally.

By the time I left PNG, seven months pregnant with our first child, Lachlan, I was on my way to living a far more purpose-centred life than I had been when I landed there nearly three years earlier. Sure, adventure travel was still important, but pursuing work that drew on my talents and served others in a meaningful way had become even more so.

Did finding a deeper sense of purpose in my life permanently eradicate all my fears? Hardly! Time and time again my fears — of not having what it takes, of failing, or looking foolish, of being rejected or exposed as inadequate or having people think I'm 'up myself' or 'too ambitious' — have risen up and tempted me to play small and safe. But my passion for my work has helped me rise above those fears — to be brave in those moments when I felt anything but. Helping others be braver, to live their own purpose and fulfil their unique potential, became the new metric for which I wanted to measure my life.

WORK FOR A PURPOSE, NOT FOR APPLAUSE

Just as a boat under power can handle any size wave if perpendicular to it, there is little you can't do if you have a purpose you believe in. While there's no one pathway for discovering your life purpose, there are many ways you can gain deeper insight into yourself, and a larger perspective on what you have to offer the world. This can make all the difference as you look ahead at what you'd love to do with the rest of your precious life.

Since leaving Papua New Guinea in the late 1990s, my professional path has been anything but linear. I've had to restart my career/calling/ business (they're all wrapped up together) on multiple continents as we moved around the world with Andrew's career — from Moresby back to Melbourne, over to Adelaide, off to Dallas, Texas, weeks after 9/11, then up to Washington, DC, back Down Under, up to Singapore, now back to the USA, though this time on our terms.

Sometimes it's been tough going. Yet whenever I've considered just throwing it all in and 'getting a job', I've always circled back to the same place ... that is (and indulge me in the double negative) — I cannot *not* do what I do. Such is the pull of my calling.

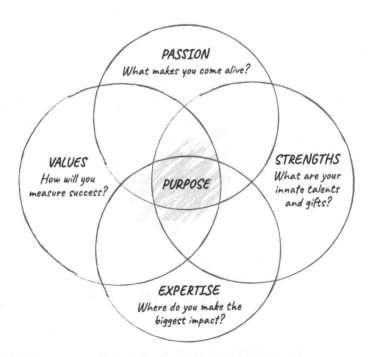

Figure 2: finding purpose in work

Four questions follow (as illustrated in figure 2) to help you find the 'sweet spot' that rests in the intersection between what you care about, what you can contribute and what will be valued most from you:

Passion — What makes you come alive?

Strengths — What are your innate talents and gifts?

Expertise — Where do you make the biggest impact?

Values — How will you measure success?

WHAT GIVES YOU ENERGY AND MAKES YOU COME ALIVE?

My two youngest sons, Matthew and Ben, were fortunate enough to be taught by Emmy Bocek when they were in kindergarten. While Emmy had been teaching rambunctious kindergarteners for 30-odd years by the time I met her, she had no shortage of energy or passion for a classroom of noisy little humans. Emmy told me once that she believed she had the 'best job in the world'. This was self-evident from both her enthusiasm and patience. I was always grateful for her passion (almost as much as I was that I didn't have to manage a classroom of kids every day — my own four were plenty!).

Over the years I've met many people from all walks of life who feel passionate about their work. From sheep farmers and chefs to scientists and beauticians — while how they spend their days spans the spectrum, they all had a passion for what they did that brought meaning to their days and, as research shows, will most likely add years to their life.

So, what makes you come alive? I'm not referring to taking your dream holiday or watching your team win the game. I'm talking about a *why* that moves up the food chain from being about you to being about something bigger than you. It's about connecting with what you feel passionate about, knowing that when you focus your attention and effort on something that puts a fire in your belly — that draws on your innate talents — you will have an invaluable and unique influence on all those your work impacts.

There's no reason to feel daunted. You don't have to declare at this point that you want to cure cancer, invent the next iPhone or solve the world's energy problems (though you might). This is about doing something that lights a spark and inspires you in some way. In fact the word 'inspire' comes from the Latin *inspirare*, which means 'to breathe or blow into'. So when you think about something that really lights you up, you will feel a sense of 'new life' breathing … awakening … within you.

For instance, my friend Ron Kaufman has a passion for uplifting service. In fact he wrote a book with that title. Yet his passion for service is far more than a commercial venture. Ron lives and breathes what it means to be of service in the world — it permeates every part of his life. You cannot be in Ron's presence without feeling lifted up and cared for. As Ron shared on my podcast, his whole life is about putting the heart of others at the heart of what he does.

So what about you — what do *you* care about? If you don't feel a burning passion that's totally fine. In which case, just think about what makes you feel that bit more alive than you might otherwise. Whatever it is … move towards it. Passion is just a word. It's the energy you feel that matters.

When I returned to study Psychology in my late 20s I had no idea my work would evolve as it has — to coaching, keynote speaking, writing books and sharing insights as a 'media commentator'. Yet as I have discovered, when you move in a direction that calls to you — that gives you energy vs sapping it from you — new horizons of possibility open up that you could never have imagined had you stayed where you were. As Martin Luther King Jr once said, 'You don't have to see the whole staircase, just take the first step.'

WHAT ARE YOUR INNATE STRENGTHS?

In *The Element*, Sir Ken Robinson wrote that our element is the point at which natural talent and skill meets personal passion. When people are in their 'element' they are both more productive and successful.

Your task here is to identify the things you've always been good at, sometimes making you wonder why other people find them so hard. Are you able to see patterns and opportunities amid complexity and uncertainty that others can't? Are you an amazing listener who is able to take in different perspectives and synthesise a way forward? Are you naturally creative, adept at finding 'out of the box solutions'? Are you a natural-born rebel with an ability to identify where the status quo needs disrupting? Are you brilliant in the details, able to execute with a precision that others find tedious? Are you a natural deal-maker, technocrat, diplomat or entrepreneur?

Of course you may not have sharpened the strengths to the extent required to achieve your boldest goals. But that doesn't mean you lack anything but practice. The good news here is that most people do not aspire towards ambitions for which they have no real talent (and those who do tend to gravitate to televised talent shows).

The flipside is also true.

I've always been uncannily good at mental arithmetic. Maybe from my years working in a milk bar serving meat pies and making shakes, and later in pubs pouring beers, where I could add up the amount due faster in my head than on a register. But I've never had any interest in pursuing a career that involved focusing on numbers. As you might guess, people are my passion. That said, I'd have enjoyed being a professional singer — think Barbra Streisand meets Lady Gaga. But a marked absence of Barbra-Gaga-like talent meant that was not to be. While I did spring a surprise song on Andrew at our wedding, our kids will happily assure you their mother was never destined for the shortlist of *A Star Is Born*.

> In this age of perfectionism, it's all too easy to get lured into the falsehood that you have to be 'the best' — the best consultant, the best sales rep, the best engineer, the best designer, the best writer. Not true! It's not about being *the* best but being *your* best. Does that mean you'll sometimes wish you were better? Of course you will. But by letting go of comparisons and consistently giving the best you can on the good days and not-so-good, you'll eventually arrive at a point that you'll realise how little reason you ever had to doubt your one-of-a-kind value in your workplace and the world.

WHERE DOES YOUR EXPERTISE MAKE THE GREATEST IMPACT?

Knowing your strengths and where you can add the most value — through the application of your education, skills, knowledge and experience — can help you focus on the opportunities, roles and career paths where you are most likely to succeed and therefore find the greatest sense of accomplishment and contribution.

Too often we undervalue the expertise we naturally acquire over time. If you reframe the concept of adding value through the lens of 'problem solving', you can home in on where you can make the greatest impact for others — whether by offering solutions to problems or finding better ways to fulfil unmet needs (or, as Steve Jobs did, inventing technology that fills needs people didn't even know they had!).

It was this exercise that inspired me to start running my public Live Brave programs and women's retreats (though with dancing and champagne, the word 'retreat' is probably not the best descriptor). While there are many great women's leadership and personal development programs available for people to attend all over the world, I just knew I could make a meaningful impact in an immersive program. I didn't do any market research; I just dived in. Following my intuition proved a good decision. Following yours will too.

WHAT DO YOU VALUE MOST DEEPLY AS A MEASURE OF SUCCESS?

Some can afford to give up the security of a salary to pursue a passion that doesn't pay (or at least not enough, soon enough). Many can't. But following the money and following your heart don't have to be mutually exclusive.

Chances are you have other values to consider — like giving your kids a great education or paying your mortgage — that prevent you from going full-time on something you're passionate about. But that doesn't mean you cannot still infuse your passion into your life in some way. Or that you can't treat it as a 'side hustle' in the shorter term while you get your financial house in order to fund the shortfall if you were to transition to it full time.

In the meantime, there is nothing stopping you from bringing more passion to what you do *right now*. While your current job may be a 'means to an end', *all work* holds intrinsic value. So if you can't change *what* you're doing anytime soon, change *how* you're doing it. By shifting the frame in which you view your current role, you can profoundly shift your experience of it. Doing so enables you to be the kind of person others want to be around. That in itself is meaningful.

> You don't have to be on course to becoming a Nobel Laureate to be living a noble life. What you do each day doesn't matter near as much as *how* you do it — the attitude you bring and the energy you spread. In thinking about how you can make a bigger difference, don't ignore the small daily differences you can make which, over time, add up to big ones.

In my podcast conversation with Alicia Tillman, Chief Marketing Officer at SAP, she shared how when she's facing a decision she will often put herself in the shoes of her 'future self' and ask herself, 'What would my future self want me to do right now?' Her answers reflect her deepest values, but also tap into her courage. She said this technique has never failed to move her forward.

Bold action can reshape your life, but unless it's guided by a clear sense of purpose, it can steer your life in a direction that leaves you wanting for something more. Much more. Simply committing yourself to contemplating the question, 'For the sake of what?' will not only embolden you to do more than you have until now, but will help you rise stronger from the challenges that unfold along the way. (If you haven't had one lately, it's coming.)

YOUR PURPOSE WILL UNFOLD
AND EVOLVE AS YOU DO

A verse in the Bible says that 'to everything there is a season, and a time to every purpose under the heaven'. The idea that there is a purpose for everything, and that every purpose has its time, has helped me be patient over the years as my own purpose has unfolded and evolved.

The same is true for you. The higher purpose for your life will reveal itself and evolve as you travel along your hero's journey, as new opportunities and new possibilities arise, beyond the horizon of what you can currently perceive. However, you must do your part by being in motion — working towards what fuels that spark within you, not what extinguishes it. Otherwise you risk missing opportunities because your focus will be elsewhere.

Let me close this chapter with the wisdom of a man whose vision for what 'could be' changed how we connect, communicate and come together — Steve Jobs. As he said at the Stanford commencement address in 2005, 'Have the courage to follow your heart and intuition. They somehow already know what you truly want to become. Everything else is secondary.'

2

LEAN TOWARDS RISK

The odds are better than you think

Twenty years from now you will regret far more those things you did not do than those you did. So throw off the bowlines, sail away from the safe harbor, catch the trade winds in your sails. Explore. Dream. Discover.

MARK TWAIN

When I was 21, I spent a year backpacking around the world. I'd moved back to my parents' farm after graduating university and spent five months working two jobs — sorting frozen vegetables during the day and pouring beers at a local pub at night — to fund my adventure. I'd never been overseas (with seven kids on a small dairy farm, our family vacations were road trips only) so while it was an exciting prospect, it was also slightly daunting.

My first stop was the USA.

About a month into my trip I visited a family cousin in California. Upon telling him that I would be travelling to New York City, he remarked that he thought my parents were irresponsible letting their daughter go off 'gallivanting around the world' on her own, that I was far too naive for being so bold, and that he'd never allow his daughter (just a little older than me) to do anything so foolish. 'It's far too risky,' he said.

There's no arguing — it *was* risky. Insofar as there were risks, particularly given that there were no mobile phones or even email back then, which limited my ability to call home for help if I ever needed it.

He was right. I could have been robbed, or raped, or drugged and sold into a sex-trafficking racket, or murdered.

But I wasn't.

Not even when I eventually did land in the Big Apple and got lost on my first subway ride, accidentally exiting into the bustling streets of Harlem when it was still the murder capital of America. What did I do? I went back down into the subway and headed back a few stops to where I should have got out. That experience was one of countless many that taught me how to discern risks and recognise my ability to handle situations when I landed in a place that was more dangerous than I'd reckoned on.

> Sometimes our fear of the danger is disproportionate to the *actual* danger. This doesn't mean there are not legitimate dangers that we should consider and seek to safeguard ourselves against. Rather that we should also stand guard against our tendency to overestimate the likelihood of their occurrence and underestimate how we'd handle them if they did.

Clearly there were risks to backpacking around the world as a young single woman. But time and time again I met incredibly decent and generous people who went out of their way to help me out or point me in the right direction (there was no Google Maps back then!).

By the time I arrived back in Australia 12 months later, I had well and truly caught the travel bug. Within months I was planning my next adventure — this time across the Sahara, through Central Africa and the Middle East.

Had I only focused on what could have gone wrong — on all the risks — I'd have risked missing out on what was one of the most formative experiences of my life. It not only opened my eyes to a whole world outside

Australia, but it helped me to discern smart risks from foolish ones, to finetune my inner risk radar and strengthen my 'courage muscles' for life.

Over the years I've ventured out of my comfort zone countless times, meeting people from many countries and cultures. I've learned that while we humans may live very different lives, we are ultimately far more alike than we are different. More so, that the greatest barrier we face to living the biggest lives we're capable of living is fear of what might go wrong if we dared to try.

BEWARE OF NORMALISING FEAR; NOT ALL RISKS ARE TO BE AVOIDED

Let's face it, every day you're bombarded with reasons to feel afraid. Fear of random violence, recession, terrorism, child predators, online predators, identity theft, AI, outsourcing jobs to low-wage countries … the list is long and new threats seem to sprout like poisonous mushrooms.

Marketers prey on fears. Media prey on fears. Politicians play to fears.

Fear sells products. Fear gets clicks. Fear makes profit. Fear grows power.

And fear fuels fear.

> **Elevating societal anxiety boosts the bottom line for many companies. Little wonder there are so many merchants of fear investing heavily in keeping you scared. It's why, in a culture preoccupied by risk and consumed by fear, refusing to become its pawn — discerning smart risks from foolish ones — has become ever more critical. Nowhere is this more needed than in the workplace. Nowhere will it be more rewarded.**

Fear is a primal emotion wired into your psychological DNA to protect you from harm and alert you to risk. Its sole purpose is to steer you away from situations it perceives would risk endangering your physical, mental or emotional wellbeing.

Fear can be traced back to our cave-dwelling days when spotting a potential threat to a person's safety could spell the difference between life and death. So let's be clear, fear can be a constructive emotion insofar as it alerts us to potential threats, putting us 'on the ready' for managing them. Yet the risks of the 21st century are far less about losing one's life to a predatory beast and far more about losing face in front of the people we'd like to impress.

Back in the 1980s Ulrich Beck, a professor at the London School of Economics, coined the term 'risk society' to describe countries and cultures in which people have become so hypercautious about all potential risks that they live in a constant state of fear.

Left unchecked, fear overtakes logical rational thinking. It drives us to miscalculate risks — to overreact to some potential threats and underreact to others. If I had a dollar for every time someone in the USA has told me they were too afraid to visit Australia for fear of being killed by one of Australia's deadly snakes or poisonous spiders (or sharks or crocs or jellyfish or 'drop bears' ... yes, they're a thing). As I sometimes point out, less than two people die from snakebite every year in Australia, and no-one has died from a spider bite since the 1970s. In contrast, people are 3000 times more likely to die from gun death in the USA. This is not a political statement, but a statement of fact.

> We often miscalculate risks and tend to overestimate the likelihood of a negative outcome when a potential danger captures our imagination. It's why many people are afraid of flying in planes when, in fact, they are more likely to die driving their car.

Of course you might not be the least bit fearful about boarding a plane for a 15-hour flight to Australia (or leaving Australia to backpack your way around the world). However, you may well still sometimes fall into the trap of holding off making any decision for fear of making the wrong one, all the while putting yourself at the greater risk of missing out on an opportunity because you've been sitting on the fence. Or maybe you simply fail to take the small interpersonal risks required to forge more authentic relationships, build a stronger team or grow your visibility and reputation to open more doors of opportunity.

TRUST YOURSELF, NOT YOUR FEARS

Fear limits our lives more than any external obstacle ever can. If you're wondering where it might be limiting yours, take a moment to answer these questions.

Do you avoid uncertainty wherever you can?

Does concern that you'll be 'found out' as unworthy keep you from putting yourself out there in bigger ways?

Do you spend more time conjuring up worst-case scenarios about what could go wrong than you do about what you'd like to make more right?

No-one relishes the prospect of being rejected, or having their intelligence questioned. No-one enjoys giving candid feedback they know will be confronting. No-one likes making decisions that don't turn out optimal. But unless you're willing to risk 'all the above', you'll never create a life that lights you up or discover how little reason you ever had to feel afraid to begin with.

It's a simple rule of life — you have to be willing to risk the safety of where you are now in order to create the possibilities you want most.

LEAN TOWARD RISK

Lean towards risk. This was one of the core lessons *New York Times* columnist David Brooks extracted from the hundreds of essays he received after inviting readers aged over 70 to submit their 'life reports'.

He noted that the happiest respondents were those who had taken risks in life rather than avoiding them.

Bronnie Ware, author of *The Top Five Regrets of the Dying*, found a similar sentiment during her years working as a palliative care nurse. As she shared on my *Live Brave* podcast, one of the biggest regrets most people have is that they lived too safe and risked too little. To rephrase the Greek philosopher Tacitus, the desire for safety stands against every great and noble life.

The word 'risk' often conjures up images of people engaged in physically risky activities — free divers, free solo climbers, racing-car drivers or aerial acrobats. Or of business mavericks and trailblazing entrepreneurs — such as Richard Branson and Elon Musk — ready to lay it all on the line for a high-risk venture.

But risk is not only the domain of adrenaline junkies, speed demons and trailblazers. Risk is relevant to every single one of us. Every single day. Sometimes you have to assess risk in the big decisions in life, but most of the time the risks you're confronted with are more mundane: whether to push back on the consensus thinking in a weekly team meeting, raise your hand to lead an important client presentation or project, or set a boundary with a colleague who has overstepped it. So, if avoiding risk has been your success strategy until now, I encourage you to rethink the nature of risk and how not taking risks may have kept you from achieving more of the success you want.

Let me be clear though: being willing to take risks isn't an excuse for parking your brain. Neither is it about denying or discounting legitimate risks — political, financial, strategic, operational or otherwise. Rather, it's about being willing to put yourself 'out there' when the situation calls for it, despite your fear of falling short or losing face. As Nelson Mandela said, 'The brave man is not he who does not feel afraid, but he who conquers that fear.'

This chapter is focused on adopting a mindset that embraces risk-taking as part and parcel of what is required for you to thrive and accomplish whatever it is that inspires you (or at least to exponentially expand your experience of being alive by the pursuit!).

The term 'mindset' refers to the overarching approach you bring to your life. It aligns with the work of Stanford's Professor Carol Dweck, whose book *Mindset* unpacks her research on the value and application of a 'growth mindset' as distinct from a 'fixed mindset'. The former liberates us to learn new skills and try new things. The latter stifles our ability to adapt, to grow and learn the skills necessary to flourish in all arenas of life.

Yet if it were easy to adopt a growth mindset, embracing risk-taking as indispensable for success, more people would. It's not easy because it flies against our instinctive desire for belonging, 'looking good' in the eyes of those we seek to impress and avoiding the consequences of failure.

When it comes to fulfilling your potential at work and throughout your career and life, my research has led me to conclude that there are ultimately two fundamental mindsets that separate those who thrive — in their careers, leadership, relationships and life — from those who don't.

The first mindset is fuelled by fear and drives hypercaution and risk aversion. I've dubbed this the Risk-Averse Mindset. The second is fuelled by purpose and fosters courage. I call this the Risk-Ready Mindset.

Of course, not all risks are created equal. This book is focused primarily on the social–emotional risks that stifle human potential and impede progress, not on the risks that actually protect our wellbeing and that of those we love. For instance, when my dad needed a triple heart bypass I wanted the surgeons to avoid risk. And when my husband managed a manufacturing plant where people's lives were at stake, he worked hard to mitigate the risk of harm to the employees, the surrounding community and the environment.

The irony is that when people fail to take emotional risks — like having conversations around accountability or giving upward feedback — they can inadvertently put others at more risk. For instance, the investigation into the root causes of BP's Deep Horizon oil spill in the Gulf of Mexico found that the culture was so fearful of negative upward feedback that people who knew there were serious risks of operational failure did not risk their jobs to flag them.

In short, only when you've learned how to lean towards social–emotional risk can you be fully effective in managing all the other types of risk.

YOUR BRAIN IS HARDWIRED TO KEEP YOU SAFE, NOT MAKE YOU HAPPY

Your brain is wired to protect you from pain or injury — physical, emotional, social. The interplay of a whole series of complex neurobiological factors impacts how you approach decisions and why you may sometimes hold back from taking the risks that — emotions aside — would clearly be worth taking. As brain-imaging technology has advanced, so too has our understanding of how our brains process information, assess potential risks and make decisions.

Research has found that most people are about twice as sensitive to potential losses as to potential gains, which leads to risk aversion. Using Magnetic Resonance Imaging (MRI) technology, a team of psychologists from UCLA studied how our brains evaluate the possibility of gaining versus losing when making risky decisions. Participants in their study were given $30 and then asked whether they would agree to each of more than 250 gambles in which they had a 50:50 chance of winning an amount of money or losing another amount of money. Would they, for example, agree to a coin toss in which they could win $30 but lose $20? The researchers weren't as interested in the subjects' reactions to winning or losing, but the neural activity in the parts of their brain as they decided what to do. By studying which parts of the brain activated as the amount of money participants could win or lose increased, the researchers were able to predict how risk-averse people were.

> **Neuroscience has proven that our brains are wired to overestimate the risks, to underestimate our ability to handle their consequences and to discount the cost of cautious inaction (which are most often delayed and invisible). But don't buy into the faulty logic that the 'safest option' is the one which serves your highest good. Playing it safe is not without risk and can land you in a future circumstance that offers less security than had you taken the leap.**

Regions of the brain that become more active as the amount increased are called 'reward centres'. Those who show much more neural sensitivity to losses relative to gains are the same people who are very reluctant to gamble unless they are offered extremely favourable odds. Conversely, those who are neurologically about as sensitive to losses as gains are the ones who are more willing to take a risk.

The researchers also confirmed previous findings that people are more 'turned off' by potential losses than they are 'turned on' by potential gains. This provides a neurological explanation for why so many people opt to stick in a situation they dislike (a dead-end job or dysfunctional relationship) rather than risk the possibility of landing in a worse situation. Unless they think the potential gain is going to be exceptional, they'd rather stick with the 'devil they know' than risk the 'devil they don't'.

But at what cost?

Unfortunately, many people kid themselves about the price they pay for not taking a risk. Not me or you, of course, but 'other people'. In the process, they surrender any possibility of creating a more rewarding future. Yet by talking up the risk of making a change, and discounting or denying the price of playing safe, they become complicit in their own misery.

Which hemisphere of the brain you rely on most also impacts how you assess risk. The left side of your brain is the logical, 'play it safe' side. Being more focused on probabilities than possibilities, it's the side that's most risk-averse. The right side of your brain is the 'experimental' side. It's more likely to pay attention to your feelings, engage in creative problem-solving, think outside the box and consider big-picture possibilities rather than statistical probabilities.

Neither side is superior to the other. We need both sides of our brain engaging in 'whole brain' thinking when assessing risk and making decisions. People who operate more out of the left side of their brain are more analytical when it comes to measuring and weighing up risks. They need to see the facts or run the numbers. We all know these people — the ones who create spreadsheets with an elaborate rubric to make a multi-variable cross-analysis. The result: paralysis by analysis.

Then there're those who operate more from the right brain. These folk are more likely to lean on their intuition to help them decide. Of course, as helpful as our 'inner sage' can be, sometimes we can confuse an intuitive feeling with wishful thinking. Just as operating from the left brain can lead to indecision, operating only from the right brain can lead to rash decisions.

Whichever side is your natural tendency, just know that you need to engage both. Do your homework. Run the numbers. Read the contract. Run a risk analysis using the simple Risk/Reward Matrix coming up in a few pages (see figure 3 on page 40). But then get quiet and ask yourself, 'What feels right? What inspires me most?'

> **Courage isn't comfortable. If it were, there'd be far fewer people languishing on the sidelines, settling for less than the biggest lives they're capable of living.**

LEARN TO MANAGE YOUR FEAR OR IT WILL MANAGE YOU

Several years ago, I found myself frozen on a trapeze platform in what turned out to be a humbling yet valuable lesson on the physical potency of fear. Looking up from the ground, the platform above hadn't seemed that high. But with each step up the rope ladder, the ground below felt exponentially further away. When I reached the top and looked over at the trapeze bar I was supposed to grab, fear gripped me like a vice and my body froze in terror, as though I was being asked to take a leap over a mile-deep crevasse. Sure, intellectually I knew I couldn't hurt myself. After all, I was wearing a safety harness, which was attached to safety ropes, and below me was a large safety net. Yet emotionally, that primal part of my brain was screaming 'DON'T DO IT!' as though I was free climbing up K2, doomed to plunge to certain death.

If it weren't for my friends on the ground below yelling up at me the title of my first book — 'Find your courage Margie!' — I might never have taken the leap. But fear of professional humiliation kicked in and out I leapt, a loud shriek piercing the air! (There's a fine line between exhilaration and terror.)

The experience reinforced the fact that unless we learn to manage our fear, our fear will manage us. On the upside, my day out at circus school with girlfriends reassured me that I had not missed my calling.

Neuroscience has found that our perceptions go straight to the emotional processing part of our brain (the amygdala), bypassing the thinking part of the brain (the cortex). Cortisol floods our neural pathways, marshalling us to take action: to move away from danger, to protect or defend. The amygdala triggers an automatic reflexive fear response before our cortex has the chance to fully evaluate the situation. 'Neural hijack' ensues. My experience on the trapeze platform showed just physically powerful the fear reaction can be.

It's also why one of the most powerful questions you can ever ask yourself is this:

Where am I giving fear of what I do not want the power to stop me from moving towards what I do want?

It's possible that what keeps you from really pondering this question, much less acting on your answer to it, is also fear. Fear of the risks. Fear of messing up or losing out. Fear of what others will think or say or do. Fear of hurting feelings or being judged as inadequate or just humiliating yourself. Fear of the emotions you will feel if things don't land as you want.

Embracing risk as a prerequisite for thriving — in your career, leadership, relationships and life — is key to succeeding in the bigger game of life. Those who are the biggest losers in the grand scheme of life are not those who have dared greatly and fallen short of the mark. They are those who lived so safe that they never truly lived at all.

But what if you dared to believe that what you really want is truly possible for you: what then? What if, instead of trying to avoid the emotional pain that could follow failure, you were willing to risk your comfort for the sake of something far bigger and better — for the prize of a life that was richer, fuller and more meaningful than the life you've led up until now? What if, instead of living with a Risk-Averse Mindset, you committed to living with one that embraced risk as essential to success: a Risk-Ready Mindset?

Committing to live your life fully requires acknowledging that all life is risky. Did you catch that?

ALL LIFE IS RISKY.

When you can embrace the essential truth that all of your life is risky — that nothing outside yourself is certain or guaranteed — you can liberate yourself from a life spent worrying about the 'bad things' you fear might happen, and take the risks needed to create more of the 'good things'.

While it's convenient to believe that courage is a personal attribute endowed upon the few at birth, ultimately courage is a mindset that every single person — including those who are naturally more cautious — can build. In fact, science has proven that courage is a skill and, like all skills, it can be learned and strengthened with practice.

> Neuro-imaging technology has found that our brains are twice as sensitive to potential losses as they are to potential gains. In other words, you're wired to focus more on what could go wrong than on what might go right; more on what you could lose in the short term than on what you could gain in the longer term. So whatever decision you are facing, ask yourself: what do you risk losing if you don't take the risk?

Your innate negativity bias programs you to focus more on what you don't want to happen. But each time you do that, you psychologically enlarge the holes in your imaginary safety net, amplifying low-grade concerns into full-blown terror. As I stood on that trapeze platform looking down, it was only when I decided to focus on taking flight, not falling to my death, that I could rise above my fear and take that leap.

The same is possible for you too, regardless of the situation you find yourself in.

Choosing to adopt a Risk-Ready Mindset is not a one-off decision. Choosing to be brave with your life doesn't render you permanently immune to fear or spare you ever again succumbing to cowardice. No, courage sits on a spectrum. Becoming more courageous is not a discrete event but a process. You facilitate that process each time you defy your fears and move in the direction from which courage calls, net or no net.

Some days you'll feel like you've hit the ball out of the park. You've been bold and assertive. You had that conversation you'd been putting off. You put up your hand to lead the project. You made the big ask. You stuck your neck out, risked the rejection or took that giant leap of faith over the chasm of fear and doubt. On other days … not so much. You said nothing despite how much you felt others needed to hear it. You didn't risk the ask. In fact you risked nothing.

It is part of the human condition to sometimes succumb to fear even when we intellectually know we should rise above it. But the fact that fear sometimes holds the reins in your life is far less important than what you do once you realise you've just let fear win. In that moment, taking a step back from your situation to reframe the risks, reassess the costs of not taking one and recommit to walking the braver path will change the trajectory of your future. It will not banish your fear, nor make you immune to it. But each time you decide to act in its presence, you weaken its power and strengthen your own.

WHAT YOU *THINK* YOU FEAR IS WHAT YOU *LINK* TO FEAR

Cultural anthropologist Ernest Becker wrote that people's fears are fashioned out of the ways in which they perceive the world around them. What you *think* you fear is rarely what you *really* fear. Rather, it's what you *link to* fear. It's the associations you make in your mind about what *might* happen that cause you to feel afraid. And what you think *might* happen is always based on some past event. So as you think about whether to take an action or not, drill down and ask yourself, what am I really afraid of here?

Then take a moment to acknowledge that your fear is trying to spare you from experiencing an emotion that you think will be painful. But again, what pain do you put yourself in if you stay where you are?

KNOW WHAT TO FEAR

Several years ago my husband and I decided to take our four kids, aged nine to 14 at the time, to Nepal. We've always wanted our kids to experience the world more broadly — to experience first-hand the reality of life for most of the world's population and develop a greater appreciation for the circumstances they were born into. Once in Nepal, we signed up for our first ever family whitewater rafting trip (we've since done many more). While I felt a little apprehensive at first, I figured there was nothing to be anxious about given we were all kitted out in safety gear (albeit to Nepalese safety standards!).

After the first set of rapids the kids at the front of the raft excitedly announced that we had an unpaid passenger in our midst — a snake. Despite, or maybe because of, growing up in the Aussie bush where snakes aren't uncommon, I am *not* a fan. So discovering one was slithering around the bottom of our raft put me immediately on edge.

Since I was sitting in the back of the raft, I couldn't see how big it was so my imagination quickly went into overdrive, blowing it up into king cobra–sized dimensions. After manoeuvring myself into the middle of the raft, I looked ahead downriver to see we were quickly approaching some intimidating rapids that required my full engagement — at the oars *and* closer to the snake. I had to make a choice: was this snake a greater threat or the swirling rapids and rocks? The rapids won.

On beaching our raft downriver our guides managed to catch and release the snake into the river. To my relief and bemusement, it measured no longer than a ruler and no thicker than my index finger. As it quickly disappeared downstream it brought home how often we can focus our fear on the wrong things.

Of course there is no escaping that there are legitimate risks that you are right to be cautious about. But whatever challenges and choices you are facing, be mindful that you may be channelling your fear in the wrong direction. As Plato said over two millennia ago, 'Courage is knowing what not to fear.'

In *The Gift of Fear*, personal security expert Gavin de Becker writes, 'Far too many people are walking around in a constant state of vigilance, their intuition misinformed about what really poses danger.' Genuine fear is a signal intended to be very brief. It's a servant of your intuition. But too often fear about what you don't want to happen gets in the way of pursuing and accomplishing what you do.

Not only that, but if you're feeling fearful all the time, there's little or no capacity left for those times when fear is genuinely needed. As de Becker writes, 'Precautions are constructive, whereas remaining in a state of fear is destructive.' Rock climbers will tell you it isn't the mountain that kills, it's the panic.

> Like every emotion, fear is contagious. The more often you feel fear, the more pervasive it becomes in your life. Left unchecked, it can set up permanent residence in your psyche, tainting every perception and cutting you off from your courage. The more often you hand the reins of your life over to your fear — rational or not — the more real estate it occupies in your psyche until, without you realising it, it can dominate the emotional landscape of your life and hold your happiness hostage. But you choose otherwise. It's why, in today's culture of fear, where people obsess daily over risks, you have to be vigilant not to let fear call the shots and to take action in its presence. It's why living bravely is indispensable for living well.

As the Stoic Seneca wrote way back when, 'There is nothing so certain in our fears that's not yet more certain in the fact that most of what we dread comes to nothing.'

TAME FEAR-CASTING

We've all felt a bit like the lion tamer who put an advertisement in the local paper: 'Lion tamer wants tamer lion'. Of course you can never completely 'tame' your fears. Nor would you want to. Fear serves an important purpose. But in today's climate of fear, we must discern those fears that are serving us from those which are keeping us stuck, stressed out and unnecessarily scared. As Dr Phil McGraw shared with me in an interview about 're-entry fear' as the world moves out of the COVID-19 pandemic, 'Monsters live in the dark.'

Important in taming fear is to notice when you're letting your imagination hijack rational thought and get the better of you (literally and figuratively). In times of uncertainty, we are prone to turning our forecasts into fearcasts, conjuring up all array of catastrophic scenarios in your imagination just as I did with that little snake.

Just as my fear enlarged the holes in the safety net at the trapeze school, sometimes your fear has you picturing yourself living out of a shopping cart on welfare as you contemplate changing jobs. Or perhaps your imagination has you being marched out of the building for daring to speak up and challenge your boss on an issue. Taming fear isn't just about growing your competence at whatever challenge you'd like to take on. It's also about increasing your competence for reeling in the horror movie in your head.

The best way to end the horror movie is to refocus on the movie you want to be producing: mentally painting an inspiring vision of yourself successfully enjoying the outcome you *do* want. If you have a particular image that keeps cropping up whenever you think about doing something bold—whether speaking up to your boss and asking for a pay rise or starting your own business—observe the link between the image and what you fear. Only when you start to 'unlink' those associations—often reinforced by the hyped-up fear-laden headlines blaring around you—will you loosen the grip your fear has on you and tame it back into submission … until next time.

REFRAME RISK; TURN FEAR INTO AN ALLY

We humans are more motivated by the avoidance of pain than the pursuit of pleasure. As such, we can harness the emotional potency of fear as a powerful and positive motivating force by shifting our attention from what we fear might happen if we take a risk to what we should fear if we don't take the risk. So whatever decision you're facing, fast forward a year into the future and get present to the price you will pay if you don't take the risk. Our psychological immune systems can justify an excess of courage over an excess of cowardice. Fear regret more than failure.

By reframing the risks, you harness the power of fear to your benefit. The Hebrew word *yirah* means both 'to fear' and 'to see'. *Yirah* teaches that life's essential choice is to open your eyes to available opportunities, or to fear the consequences of avoiding that reality. So when you become fully aware of the often-profound cost of *not* acting, you harness the energy of fear to motivate you away from unwanted consequences or situations and towards the outcome or goal you do want.

Too often we disregard or downplay the impact that fears can have on the decisions we make. This can keep you from taking the bold actions required to take your work to the next level or use your strengths to drive impact on a whole new level. When your actions are confined to the limits of your comfort zone, your results will also be limited.

Fear regret more than failure. It's easier to justify excess courage than excess cowardice.

Leslie Sarasin was 24 when she quit her secure job working at a seafood company in San Diego to move across the continent to pursue a more rewarding career. 'There's a fine line between stupidity and bravery,' Sarasin told me, 'but there are times you have to be willing to walk it if you want to create a rewarding career.'

At the time she was aware that she was taking a risk, but she felt the bigger risk was staying where she was: in a job that held little opportunity to grow into bigger roles where she could make a bigger impact. She recalled that her father didn't speak to her for months afterwards, but she was determined that she wouldn't look back with regret.

That one brave move set her career on a whole new trajectory, eventually taking her into the role of CEO of the Food Marketing Institute. Representing about 1500 companies in 50 countries worldwide, Sarasin has learned to trust her instincts: 'Sometimes you have to do what's right for you, even if it's not popular or offers no guarantee of success.'

DON'T DISCOUNT THE COST OF CAUTIOUS INACTION

Making choices requires wrestling with trade-offs between the pros and cons of one course of action (which is often doing nothing) against another. Too often, though, when we compare our list of pros against cons for each option, we make invalid comparisons based on the false assumption that the present situation will remain the same. As President Kennedy once said, 'There are risks and costs to a program of action. But they are far less than the long-range risks and costs of comfortable inaction.'

Professor Philip Bobbitt from the University of Texas called this human tendency the Parmenides fallacy, named after the Greek philosopher who argued that the world is static and that all change is an illusion. Of course in reality nothing remains static; the present state is an ongoing process of evolution and change. When you try to justify to yourself that not taking an action because it may result in failure is riskier than doing nothing, you need to keep in mind the risks associated with doing nothing. Usually things that aren't working well only get worse. Doing nothing doesn't mean that nothing will change about the present situation, because it will continue to evolve. Or — perhaps more likely — deteriorate. So, when assessing risk, you have to consider what will happen if you don't take the risk.

In an effort to take the safest path possible, many people end up living a life they would never consciously have chosen. Just look around you at people who have avoided risk all their lives and observe the shape of their lives.

So to help you in deciding whether you should take a risk, work through each of the four quadrants in my Risk/Reward Matrix, shown in figure 3 (overleaf). Remember, we often tend to put a disproportionate amount of energy onto the costs of taking a risk and discount the costs we pay for not taking the risk — this will help you avoid that innate bias.

Nothing worthwhile has ever been achieved with a guarantee of success. Nothing ever will be.

	POTENTIAL COSTS	POTENTIAL BENEFITS
TAKE THE LEAP	· I will have to work hard · I'll have less time for leisure or other people · It will be scary, emotionally uncomfortable and inconvenient · I'll have to live with uncertainty and risk, making mistakes and imperfect decisions	· I will be learning new skills and building marketable expertise · I'll be meeting new people, building reputation and gaining exposure to decision-makers · I will grow confidence for bigger undertakings and feel more alive in my life

RISK / REWARD MATRIX

	POTENTIAL COSTS	POTENTIAL BENEFITS
PLAY IT SAFE	· I will have to live with 'What if I'd tried?' · I won't be growing, learning, meeting new people, building new skills, growing my reputation · Life will continue on much as it is except that what is frustrating me now will likely only get worse · My future will be much of the same	· I don't have to deal with any more uncertainty, inconvenience and stress · I don't risk tarnishing my 'winning' reputation · I avoid upping the ante on my already busy daily juggling act · I don't have to bother learning new skills or meeting new people

Figure 3: the Risk/Reward Matrix

LIFE REWARDS ACTION, NOT INDECISION

Courage is far less about heroism on the battlefield or in the midst of a natural disaster and far more about the everyday choices you make as you navigate your way through life. It's not the absence of fear (or doubt or misgivings) about your ability to succeed. It's action in the presence of fear. In the words of John Wayne, 'Courage is being scared to death but saddling up anyway'.

When you engage with life through a Risk-Averse Mindset, your decisions are guided more by fear. This narrows your repertoire of potential actions which, in turn, narrows the experiences you have and the opportunities you create and ultimately shrinks your life and your confidence with it.

In short, the fewer risks you take, the less comfortable you grow taking any risks.

On the flipside, when you approach life with a Risk-Ready Mindset, it breeds confidence and compels you to step outside your comfort zone. In turn, you generate opportunities and outcomes that expand your capacity for bigger challenges and greater endeavours.

Believe it or not, this is true whether or not you land the perfect outcome.

Hear me out.

While I was spending time with Richard Branson, he spoke a lot about the importance of a balance between managing the downside of risks while learning how to 'fail forward'. 'You can prepare for every eventuality but there will always be something which will knock you off balance,' Branson says. 'There are some risks which don't pay off as you thought they would.'

If you've never heard of Virgin Cola, there's a reason for that. Launched in 1994 in New York to great fanfare, this is one of Branson's risks that did not pay off. Yet in the wake of the failure, he was determined to make sure he extracted every bit of learning he could from it.

'We wanted to smash our way past the competition,' he says. 'However, it turned out we hadn't thought things through — declaring war on Coke was madness.'

Up until that point, Virgin had been a disruptor brand, entering new markets, shaking up the norm and providing a stronger value proposition than its competitors. 'But we'd forgotten one thing,' he says. 'We only do business where we can offer consumers something brilliantly different. Virgin Cola just wasn't different enough. Although the business ultimately failed, it was a great learning experience.'

Even when your risk-taking doesn't land you the outcome you wanted, you're still better off for having taken the risk because you were in action, you were learning, you were meeting people, you were discovering what didn't work, you were building your brand, and you were finetuning your ability to discern smart risks from foolish ones, all the while growing your 'courage muscles' for life.

> Sure, when you take a risk, you might sacrifice comfort, time or money. However, that pales against what you sacrifice when you play too safe — discovering what works, what doesn't and what you're truly capable of doing. When you stick with the status quo you cut off the possibility of learning, of growing, of creating, of winning and of experiencing the aliveness that comes from bravely stepping from the stands into the arena of life.

You would not get these benefits if you stuck with cautious inaction. As Daniel Gilbert wrote in *Stumbling on Happiness*, our psychological immune system can more easily justify an excess of courage than an excess of cowardice.

In short, daring to be brave in what you do will always put you in a better position over the longer haul of your life than living in fear-laden excuses and justifications.

> Neuroscientists have found that cells that fire together, wire together. The more often you engage in activities that are courageous, the more adept you'll become at them. You don't have to start with the most nail-biting act of courage. Sure, think big and aim high. But right now, focus on the choices right in front of you. Fear is contagious, but so too is courage. It's like a muscle. The more often you choose to do the brave thing, the braver you become.

If you want to make a big change, start with a series of smaller ones. Had I started on the trapeze at ground level, and then gradually worked my way up to the full height of the trapeze platform, I would have most likely not been so terrified when I tried my first jump. Likewise, if you want to step into a management role (or any role with greater responsibility), start by putting your hand up for opportunities that will build your skillset and confidence at management tasks.

EMBODY THE BRAVE-HEARTED PERSON YOU ASPIRE TO BECOME

Fear is physical. If you've ever felt afraid, you know that it wasn't just a feeling in your head; it was in your body: in the tightness of your throat, the sick feeling in your stomach, or the sweat on your brow and the palms of your hands.

I recall my first interview with the *Today* show at NBC's studios overlooking New York's iconic Rockefeller Plaza. I was so nervous that my teeth were chattering and my legs trembling as I sat down on the stool beside Kathie Lee Gifford. No-one seemed to notice how nervous I was but I vividly recall pursing my lips together in the seconds prior to the interview going live to avoid looking like an idiot in front of *Today*'s few million-odd viewers. Fortunately, as so often happens, when the cameras started rolling, my focus on saying what it was that I wanted to convey to viewers distracted me from my anxiety and off I went. I've had similar experiences many times, either doing live TV or speaking to audiences from a stage.

> Overcome the physical manifestations of fear by focusing attention on the thoughts you want to feel and the person you want to be in that moment. Then move your posture, expression, language and actions into alignment. When you shift how you hold yourself physically, it shifts how you feel mentally and emotionally.

The great surrealist artist Salvador Dalí was described by his fellow students at the Madrid Art Academy as 'morbidly' shy, according to his biographer Ian Gibson. He had a great fear of blushing and his shame about being ashamed drove him into solitude. It was his uncle who gave him the sage advice to become an actor in his relations with the people around him. He instructed him to pretend he was an extrovert and to act like an extrovert with everyone, including his closest companions. Dalí did just that to disguise his mortification. Every day he went through the motions of being an extrovert and, eventually, he became celebrated as the most extroverted, fearless, uninhibited and gregarious personality of his time. He became what he pretended to be. Likewise, when you behave as the person you aspire to become, you will eventually become that person.

Research by Amy Cuddy at Harvard University has validated what many have long intuitively known: that your physical state has a direct and immediate impact on your emotional and mental state. Cuddy's research showed that moving into what she coined a 'power pose' releases hormones in your body that generate feelings of greater strength, confidence and power. She found that brief nonverbal displays of power stimulate the release of testosterone — the hormone that links to power and dominance in animals and human beings alike — which lowers the levels of cortisol, the 'stress' hormone that can undermine your ability to think, speak and act in a calm, clear-headed and confident way.

Cuddy's research found that you express power through open, expansive postures, and express powerlessness through closed, contractive postures. In short, putting yourself into a 'power pose' not only makes you think and feel more powerful (and courageous!) but changes your actual physiology and, subsequently, your actions. Even just changing the expression on your face can alter your mental and emotional state. Indeed, studies have found that by simulating facial expressions we take on the emotions those facial expressions portray. That is, even if you don't feel like smiling, when you smile, you ultimately feel happier and friendlier. It's not just psychological; it's physiological. Likewise, if you furrow your eyebrows and frown, you will eventually feel more angry, forlorn and depressed. In another study, researchers asked participants to make different facial expressions while being asked a question. Those who were asked to smile were more likely to agree to the request being made than those who were asked to keep a serious facial expression. Such is the power of a smile!

Fashion designer Diane von Furstenberg once said, 'I didn't know what I wanted to do, but I knew the person I wanted to be.' This echoes the words of comedian Lily Tomlin, who said, 'I always wanted to be "somebody"; I should have been more specific.'

Who do you want to be in your workplace, your industry, your life? Think of the attributes which you'd really love to embody more fully at this point in your life. Here's a few below to get you thinking.

Courageous, authentic, tenacious, resilient, focused, confident, assertive, bold, disciplined, determined, encouraging optimistic, approachable, kind, self-expressed, adventurous, daring, passionate, purposeful, tolerant, inclusive, playful, engaged.

Then write them down following the two words 'I am ...' and put them somewhere you'll see often. For instance, 'I am focused, courageous and tenacious' or 'I am resilient, confident and bold'. It may feel a bit awkward at first, but this simple exercise is deceptively powerful. Then, when you find yourself feeling frustrated, anxious or 'triggered' in any way, ask yourself what would I do right now if I were being [fill in your 'power virtues']? However you answer the question, it will indicate the action you need to take to move towards whatever it is that inspires you most.

Now lift your chin up, put a confident yet determined look on your face, look people directly in the eye with your shoulders back, feel the ground firmly beneath your feet and then step forward with a confident and purposeful stride. Practise it — sometimes you have to 'fake it 'til you make it'. By shifting how you hold yourself physically, you shift how you feel emotionally.

Hand in hand with behaving as the person you aspire to become is dressing as the self-assured and self-expressed person you aspire to be. While it may sound superficial to some, what you wear impacts not just how others perceive you, but your actual performance. In a study at Northwestern University, researchers had subjects wear white coats while performing a test that measured attention. One group was told they had on doctors' coats; the other, painters' coats. Subjects in the first group outperformed those in the second by nearly 30 per cent, suggesting that the effect our clothes have on us may be even more powerful than we thought. That is, people who dress for success not only leave a positive impression, but have greater confidence to take the actions needed to create more success.

Sure, we are living in a time of tremendous change and uncertainty. But the truth is that we've always been living with change and uncertainty. And we always will be.

> Mustering your courage to lay your vulnerability on the line for the sake of a nobler cause is the ultimate act of heroism. It's also something you have the opportunity to do every single day.

So let me ask you this:

If you were going to make a bet on yourself, what would you do?

What would you say?

What would you stop doing?

What would you let go?

Who would you dare to become?

The scariest and most exciting thing I'd ever done was deciding to buy an around-the-world ticket and leave everything and everyone I knew behind, with only a handful of traveller's cheques and a badly fitting backpack when I was 21. Yet by the time I returned home a year later, what had once scared me no longer did. I was ready to spread my wings to more foreign places. And I was smarter at being able to discern a smart risk from a foolish one.

Over the years I've travelled to more than 60 countries (and counting … I'm not done yet!). And while I appreciate that bad things could have happened, they never did.

The reality is that most of the bad things we spend our lives trying to avoid are actually low probability. To quote Mark Twain: 'I am an old man and have known a great many troubles, but most of them never happened.'

Don't let your fear of the 'troubles' that might happen keep you from pursuing whatever tugs most at your heart. Sure, playing safe can fuel a short-term sense of security but in the long march of your life, it's only by diving deep into life that you can unlock the courage dormant within you and ever feel truly secure.

So rethink risk. Lean into discomfort. And dare to take the leap … the odds are better than you think.

3

BE TRUSTWORTHY

Align bold action with right action

It often requires more courage to dare to do right than to fear to do wrong.

ABRAHAM LINCOLN

I used to work out in a bright canary-yellow Livestrong singlet. The phrase 'live strong' resonated with me and I admired Lance Armstrong, the 'super athlete' who started the Livestrong Foundation and who, for a time, embodied what it meant to live bravely.

The foundation still exists but it's long since parted ways with Armstrong, who was forced to resign when he was exposed for drug cheating. I'm still sad about it. About him … or perhaps more accurately, his lack of integrity and moral courage.

Armstrong's fall was as steep as it was sudden. As news made the airwaves of his titles (including seven consecutive Tour de France wins) being stripped and erased from the record books, I was saddened that his courage had not been matched by his character. His lack of integrity wounded us all. It also held an invaluable lesson — without integrity, nothing works.

Deciding to be braver with your life can transform your day-to-day experience of life and alter its trajectory. But if your big dreams and bold actions are not built on a rock-solid foundation of integrity, your efforts will ultimately unravel. It's rarely pretty — Armstrong's shattered legacy is a case in point.

Of course, it's easy to do the right thing when the right thing doesn't cost or inconvenience you in any significant way. It's not as easy when it requires giving up something that you value: time, recognition, money, power, information, opportunity or some other material or psychological pay-off.

> **Your commitment to living the highest vision for your life requires living in alignment with your deepest values: doing what's right ahead of what's convenient or comfortable. No amount of bravery or brilliance will compensate for a lack of integrity.**

NEVER SURRENDER SELF-RESPECT TO SELF-INTEREST

William Edwards Deming — the guru of process integrity who revolutionised manufacturing processes in the Japanese automobile industry in the 1950s — taught that it's no good doing all of the right things some of the time or some of the right things all of the time. Excellence in process integrity means doing *all* of the right things *all* of the time. It was Deming's belief that if the resulting output from a process wasn't at the desired standard, the problem might not be in the execution, but in any of the preceding steps.

When you don't like the 'output' in any aspect of your career or business, it will pay you to look back and identify which decisions and actions you took along the way that may have contributed to the less-than-satisfactory result. While you may not have done anything blatantly dishonest, it's possible that you acted in ways that lacked strength of character or which simply failed to build and maintain the trust of your important stakeholders.

You don't have to look too far to find examples of other people whose failure to act with character caused enormous harm to them and others, particularly those they care about most. The news is too often littered with tales of politicians corrupted by power, and unscrupulous corporate leaders, once hailed as trailblazers, whose reputations and careers faded out quickly as their unethical behaviour was uncovered.

Were these people always lacking in character, or did they gradually forfeit self-respect for self-interest? I say the latter. I'm sure Lance Armstrong never set out to cheat his way into the record books. No-one sets out to become corrupt and deceitful. Rather, they do so with a thousand surrenders of self-respect for self-interest. Eventually every choice they're confronted with becomes so muddied by all that has preceded that they lose all sense of right and wrong, moral and immoral. Ultimately a person without character belongs to whatever can make a captive of them, often through the false sense of security gained by acquiring more money, status or power.

Johann Wolfgang von Goethe said, 'Character develops in the stream of life.' It can also be lost in the pursuit of status, wealth and power. As you climb up the company ladder and progress in your career, the pressure to perform becomes greater, the line between black and white grows blurrier, opportunities to deceive more numerous and the temptation to cover up more alluring. As this happens, the stakes grow larger and the fall harder.

Power can put even the most ardent truth-teller to the test. But character is much easier kept than recovered; a good reputation lost is often lost forever. Which is why it's so important to commit to doing the daily work of ensuring that you never compromise yours.

Theodore Roosevelt said, 'Character in the long run is the decisive factor in the life of an individual and nation alike.' Yet in recent years we've seen an assault on character as we've witnessed behaviour from people in the highest positions of power that we'd have considered utterly unacceptable not so long ago. From crass name-calling to outright lying, the bar has been lowered as uncivil and outright deceitful behaviour has grown increasingly normalised. Yet while we cannot change the character of others, we can model the integrity we'd like to see more of.

The Edelman Trust Barometer has shown a steep decline in the trust we place in those charged to lead us over recent years. This is all the more reason why each of us who are committed to living a life rooted in decency and anchored to integrity need to pay close attention to how we conduct ourselves in every aspect of our lives. To quote Warren Buffett, 'Trust is like the air we breathe. When it's present, nobody really notices. But when it's absent, everybody notices.'

Now if you're feeling at all defensive as you read, please don't think that I'm implying that you are not a decent person. Not at all. However, I invite you to do a little 'self-audit' and identify where you could up the ante a little more on how you're engaging in the world through the lens of character, trust and integrity.

Integrity transcends simple honesty. It requires holding ourselves to the highest standards of character, decency and truth. From following through on a relatively unimportant promise to refusing to dilute the truth to minimise the fallout — integrity requires us to do what's right, even when it comes at a cost. Yet it is the only path upon which we can never get lost.

Living with integrity is akin to weeding a garden. You know that weeding is good for it, but you don't always see the results of your effort. It's only when you fail to dig out the weeds that they eventually take over.

Eventually your garden will become so riddled with weeds that no flowers will be able to blossom.

Your life – and how you conduct yourself in your career, business, relationships, finances — is no different. You have to take time to tend to those patterns of thought and behaviour that can, left unchecked, cause you to act in ways that may lack integrity — however seemingly insignificant — and slowly, gradually, leave you living out of alignment with your deepest values.

A LACK OF TRUST EXACTS A STEEP HIDDEN TAX

Trust is the glue that holds relationships, teams and organisations together. Yet it's fragile in nature; highly vulnerable to being quickly damaged. And yet, without trust, it is impossible to build the influence, make the difference or achieve the success you aspire to. At the heart of trust is the confidence — or lack thereof — we have in ourselves and in our own integrity, and in others and their commitment to doing what's right even when it costs them.

> **As you race along juggling competing priorities and managing expectations, it's all too easy to justify a little shortcut here and a white lie there. 'No big deal,' we can tell ourselves. Yet, over time those seemingly small compromises can become so habitual that we are unable to recognise how they are tarnishing our reputation and devaluing the currency of trust in our relationships.**

Before people will trust the message, they must trust the messenger. It's why a deficit of trust acts like a 'hidden tax' — undermining the quality of our conversations, blocking the flow of information, stifling collaboration, impeding productivity, and ultimately limiting the outcomes of our individual and collective efforts. A lack of trust acts like sand in the elaborate network of interactions and relationships that makes up the fabric of every working group of any size. As Professor John Whitney from Columbia Business School observed, 'Mistrust doubles the cost of doing business.' The long-term impact can be lethal.

When anyone breaches trust it leaves everyone worse off. This is as true at the interpersonal level as it is at the organisational level. When others don't trust you, they don't extend you invitations and opportunities to learn and connect and grow and progress. Likewise, when you don't trust others, you withhold information that could be valuable to them. Distrust can kill relationships before they ever get off the ground.

THE FOUR DOMAINS OF TRUST

Countless times people have shared with me their doubts about their ability to trust a person they work with — concerns which the person in question is totally unaware of. Building your awareness around the four core domains of trust — competence, sincerity, reliability and compassion — will help you win and maintain trust more effectively in all your working relationships. It will also help you be more discerning when you find yourself hesitating to trust others.

All four domains of trust, as illustrated in figure 4, work together, each reinforcing the other and magnifying the perception of the other, for better or worse. When one domain is weak, it weakens them all. Staying focused on acting with integrity within each domain will enable you to build the trust you need to add the level of value you have within yourself to bring.

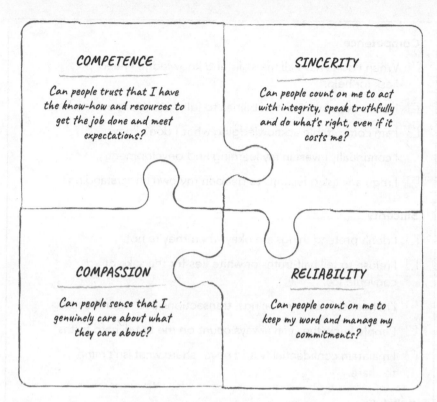

COMPETENCE

Can people trust that I have
the know-how and resources to
get the job done and meet
expectations?

SINCERITY

Can people count on me to act
with integrity, speak truthfully
and do what's right, even if it
costs me?

COMPASSION

Can people sense that I
genuinely care about what
they care about?

RELIABILITY

Can people count on me to
keep my word and manage my
commitments?

Figure 4: the four domains of trust

AUDIT YOUR TRUSTWORTHINESS

In *The 7 Habits of Highly Effective People*, Stephen Covey wrote, 'Until a person can say deeply and honestly, "I am what I am today because of the choices I made yesterday", that person cannot say, "I choose otherwise".'

This challenge consists of a series of statements that assess your 'trust-worthiness' in each of the four domains of trust: competence, sincerity, reliability and compassion. Tick those which are relatively true for you; don't tick the rest. Or, in the spirit of not playing safe, ask colleagues or friends to rate you on each domain. Invite them to be honest and to expand verbally on any domain where they can't rate you highly. That's where the value lies!

Competence

- [ ] When I don't have all the skills and knowledge I need, I ask for help.
- [ ] I don't overestimate my abilities to fulfil what's expected of me.
- [ ] I am comfortable acknowledging what I don't know.
- [ ] I continually invest in my learning and development.
- [ ] I regularly ask questions to deepen my own understanding.

Sincerity

- [ ] I don't pretend things are okay when they're not.
- [ ] I refuse to tell half-truths or white lies for the sake of convenience.
- [ ] I'm honest in all my dealings, transactions and recordkeeping.
- [ ] People know they can always count on me to tell hard truths.
- [ ] I maintain confidentiality and never share what isn't mine to share.

Reliability

- [ ] I always keep my word and honour promises. No excuses.
- [ ] I say 'no' rather than over-commit.
- [ ] I'm consistently punctual and arrive at meetings prepared.
- [ ] I get back to people when I say I will.
- [ ] I don't say 'yes' unless I know I can keep my commitment.

Compassion

- [ ] I treat everyone with respect.
- [ ] I am a good listener and ensure people feel cared for.
- [ ] People know I have a genuine interest in their wellbeing.
- [ ] I think about how my actions will impact those around me.
- [ ] I temper my candour with kindness.

COMPETENCE

Competence is the one element of trust that has firm parameters: it is task-specific. That is, you can be competent at one particular skill or area of expertise and not others. For instance, I trust my husband implicitly as a man of immense integrity. Yet I wouldn't trust him to bake a soufflé. Sure he can learn how to make a soufflé but right now, he would most likely make something closer to an omelette.

If you're putting yourself out there, taking on bigger challenges, be careful that you have the competence needed for what you want to do or that if you don't, you get the help to fill in the gaps. I've seen many careers take a steep nosedive when people have stepped into roles they were not equipped for. It's not that they didn't have the capability to learn, but they were not given, or didn't proactively pursue, the know-how, skills and support needed to earn and maintain the trust of key stakeholders.

> In most career paths it's technical competence that moves people up the first few rungs of the ladder. Yet as people advance, it's the so-called 'soft skills' (which are actually the hardest skills) that become most important. So should you find yourself in a role where you lack the competence needed to do it well, proactively seek out the training, support and advice you need to avoid damaging the trust others have put in you.

Likewise, if you want to take a bold plunge into a new role, job, industry or career, be willing to get the training and support needed to do it well. Statistics tell us that 50 per cent of businesses fail in the first five years. Often their failure boils down to the fact that the business owner didn't know what they were doing and lacked the skills and knowledge needed to build a profitable business. Being passionate is great. But it's not enough if you lack basic acumen for what you're passionate about.

On the flipside of the coin, don't underestimate your ability to learn the skills and knowledge needed to become competent in a job. This is particularly relevant for women, who are more inclined to underestimate themselves when it comes to rising to the challenges a new role will involve than their male counterparts, who are far more comfortable with just winging it.

SINCERITY

I bet you've met plenty of people who are full of hot air: whose language is so pockmarked with half-truths and exaggerations, spin and hyperbole that it seems as though they're permanently running their own infomercial. We've become so used to a diet rich in empty jargon, false flattery and hollow commitments that it's easy to think that dishonesty, deceitfulness and disingenuousness are normal — acceptable even. But in an era where so many people seem to prefer saying whatever they think others want to hear, those who are genuine, authentic and sincere make much more impact on the people around them.

Playing a bigger game in your career doesn't require stretching the truth or appeasing those more senior than you. Rather, it means having the courage to express yourself sincerely, say what you mean and mean what you say, balancing candour with kindness. Doing so will positively affect the trust you earn and the influence you ultimately wield over the course of your career.

If you're like most people you probably relish working with 'what-you-see-is-what-you-get' people. You know that they mean what they say and say what they mean — even if people don't like to hear it. They're people of their word: sincere, honest, authentic, without pretension and willing to speak the truth even when it costs them. Beyond what's obvious, you intuitively sense that there's no gap between what they really think and what they say. That said, they're not unkind or uncaring. Sincerity without caring (another pillar of character) can be cruel, so they don't say what's on their mind unless they truly believe it will serve the person they're saying it to.

When you're consistently sincere, you win the trust of your leaders, your team, your colleagues and your clients. Sincerity is a characteristic we look for in leaders and if it's lacking it undermines our trust in them more profoundly than a lack of competence, care or reliability combined. It's for this reason that when recruiting people you need to focus on character over content; on who they are as a person over what they can do (or say they can do!). You can teach skills; you can't teach character.

RELIABILITY

Debbie Kissire, former Vice Chair and Regional Managing Partner of Ernst & Young, shared with me that one thing she sees which holds capable people back in their careers is a lack of follow-through, whether on key responsibilities or the seemingly insignificant commitments made in a passing conversation. Responsible for 2500 people, Debbie said that being able to rely on someone as a 'go to' person — that is, someone who manages their time well and consistently demonstrates the tenacity, resourcefulness and reliability to get the job done — is valuable to any person in a senior role who needs to achieve their performance goals via those around them. Likewise, your ability to deliver on your commitments, and become someone others can depend on to get the job done, can open up opportunities that you may not even know exist.

Most people like to think of themselves as reliable and able to keep their word. Yet, how often have you had to wait for the same people, time and time again, before starting your meeting? And how often have you kept others waiting on you? The fact is that when you fail to keep your promises (which includes being punctual), you undermine the trust others can place in you and damage your reputation in the process. Perhaps not in a huge way. But every broken promise, even the small ones, builds on the previous one and reinforces your identity (aka brand) as someone who can't be counted on.

The natural desire to keep others happy and be agreeable makes saying no very difficult for many people. However, failing to say no when we need to can lead to overcommitment, overload and damaged relationships as we fail to fulfil promises and expectations. So before making any commitments ask yourself these questions:

Is this aligned with my top priorities, goals and values?

If I say yes to this, what will it mean (by default) saying no to?

Do I realistically have time to fulfil this commitment properly?

If saying yes to one more thing will keep you from fulfilling other commitments, then it's a matter of integrity that you say no. Offer people an alternative if you can; refer them on to someone else; negotiate a lesser commitment. But don't say yes to something unless you know you can do it. Sometimes you have to say no to the good to make room for the great.

I've yet to meet a person who would rather someone say yes and not follow through, than say no because they would not be able to keep their word.

COMPASSION

This fourth pillar of compassion (which derives from the Latin for 'co-suffering') is about 'caring about what others care about'. Yet it's more than simply feeling sorry for someone. Rather it's about actively working to support their success and ease their suffering.

People rarely care about how much you know until they know how much you care. It's why a Gallup Poll of 10 million employees around the world found that the number one reason people leave good jobs is because they don't feel their supervisor cares about them. Asked how strongly they agreed or disagreed with the statement 'My supervisor or someone I work with cares about me as a person', those who agreed were found to be more productive, contributed more to bottom-line results and stayed with their employer longer. Of course, those who didn't agree but didn't leave their job are far from productive employees.

When I interviewed Richard Branson he shared with me that if you treat people as human beings — showing you genuinely care about what they care about — it brings out the best in them. Showing genuine care about someone doesn't require donating a kidney to them. It just requires taking time to think about what is going on for them, practising empathy and putting yourself into their shoes.

As you advance in your career, how much people sense that you care about them — and by default, what they care about — impacts the depth of trust they place in you.

Robin Lineberger's story is a good case in point.

When he was a child, his airman father was shot down and killed in combat over Vietnam. Robin grew up with a strong sense of duty and a belief in the importance of working hard. He was recruited out of the US Air Force into BearingPoint's federal consulting business. He rose up through the ranks and was ultimately appointed Executive Vice President of BearingPoint.

While the business was highly successful, for a myriad reasons the firm he worked for found itself unravelling financially. A new management team was brought in to fix the problem, but Robin felt they were being short-sighted and not doing the right thing by their clients, his team of consultants or the federal business itself. So he decided to hunker down and lead his team through the turmoil, all the while seeing a large amount of his personal wealth diminish. Other industry leaders saw the writing on the wall and tried to recruit him into other executive leadership roles. Again and again Robin had opportunities to take up roles with other companies — to save his own skin — and again and again he turned them down. He refused to abandon his team of people or just walk away from the business they had built up together over more than 20 years.

As it became clear to Robin that venture-capital firms wanted to piece apart the business, he realised his 4000-plus employees would likely find themselves out of work. So he steered the negotiations to firms that valued the people and what they had built. In the end, in the worst economy in history and in the throes of bankruptcy, he managed to get all of the 4000 employees positions at Deloitte, including transferring partnership positions for many of those who had been partners already. Robin had demonstrated leadership, calm and grace under pressure and solid decision-making capability in a challenging business environment marked with mass layoffs and high unemployment. Ultimately, he was appointed CEO of Deloitte's federal business.

A humble man, Robin doesn't see himself as having done anything particularly brave. He shared with me that he just did what he felt was right, 'what any person of character would have done in the same situation'. By having character, and aligning bold action with right action, Robin won the life-long respect and loyalty of many people. (Having met a few of them, I can say that's actually an understatement. One told me he'd have followed Robin off a cliff.) When people know that you have a genuine concern for them that extends beyond how their success impacts your own, it builds trust and wins loyalty in ways that nothing else can. To quote Mark Twain: 'Always do right. This will gratify some people and astonish the rest.'

> Compassion isn't just something you feel, it's what you do. It is a positive emotion that allows us to show we care and want to help. In many ways it is love in action and in today's workplace, it's the glue that binds connection on the deepest level. When people intuitively sense that your care for them extends beyond how their success impacts your own, it builds trust in ways that nothing else can.

I recall my client Sophie telling me how little compassion her boss showed when her mother had been undergoing treatment for cancer. Every week for six months Sophie was flying interstate to be with her mother, yet not once did her boss ever ask how her mother was doing. Sophie said it didn't stop her working hard, or giving her best, but it did impact her sense of loyalty to her manager and her company. She has since left the company to work with a competitor. Had Sophie felt greater concern from her manager, perhaps that company may have retained her talent and dedication.

How much you care for those around you will filter into every conversation, every interaction and negotiation. As it does, it will influence — in both subtle and profound ways — your ability to drive positive change, foster synergies and unlock collective potential.

YOU WILL ONLY GO AS HIGH AS YOUR ROOTS GO DEEP

If you think of those you admire the most, they have coupled courage with character. Likewise, in the long arc of your life, your actions will speak far more loudly about who you were as a person than how high you climbed. Consistently acting with integrity in what you say and do — from day to day, from person to person, from situation to situation — will take you along a path upon which you can never get lost.

If you have to choose between a ladder and a compass as you navigate your life and leadership journey, choose the compass. Sure, a ladder can be helpful, but it can also have you spending your entire life climbing up the wrong wall. A compass, however, will keep you moving towards your own 'true north'.

So if you find yourself searching for ways to justify veering off the path of integrity, acting in ways that chip away at your own sense of trust-worthiness, remember that you will always, inevitably, reap what you sow. Sometimes the rewards for doing what is right over what is easier take longer to blossom, but never doubt how high you can soar over the course of your life when you are deeply grounded in integrity.

PART II
WORKING COURAGE

―――――――

UNLOCK DORMANT POTENTIAL

*The desire for safety stands against every great
and noble endeavor.*

TACITUS

4

SPEAK BRAVELY

Embrace the discomfort of crucial conversations

The truth is the kindest thing we can give folks in the end.

HARRIET BEECHER STOWE

Ever held your tongue, said nothing, kept the peace and avoided an awkward conversation only to regret it later?

Most of us have.

The most important conversations are often the least comfortable.

I know this to be an inconvenient truth because, while I'm loath to admit it, there's been more than one occasion in my life when I've chickened out of an important conversation. The emotional discomfort of addressing an issue has kept me from raising it.

Every time, I come to regret my lack of courage.

One time that stands out most was early in my professional career working for a large multinational. A year into a sought-after marketing role with 'fast-track upward potential' (their words, not mine), I resigned. The work environment in my team had become so toxic and my co-workers, all older but less senior than me, had been so mean to me (yes, I know it sounds very childish in hindsight) since day one that I decided I could bear it no longer and quit. It was only on my last day at work, when I was asked to meet with the divisional head, that I found the courage to say anything, to speak my truth. When I answered his question about why I was leaving, given I'd only come on board a year earlier, he said, 'I wish you'd come to me. Then I could have done something about it.'

Aargh … the cost of cowardice. In this case, my own. I could defend myself by saying that I was young and inexperienced — I was. But that doesn't change the outcome. My fear of an awkward conversation had kept me from any conversation and cut off the possibility of improving the situation. It was a poignant lesson.

Chances are that you also can think of times when you've avoided a tough conversation only to regret it later.

Too awkward. Too uncomfortable. Too risky.

So you said nothing (well, at least not directly to someone who could have done something about it) and the situation got worse. Maybe much worse. Maybe so bad that it got past the point of any redemption.

Maybe you quit like I did, or walked out, or lost your temper, or grew an ulcer.

It happens.

> **When it comes to speaking up about issues that can weigh us down or open new doors, delay grows increasingly expensive.**

Windows of opportunity close. Tensions rise. Hurts fester. Mistrust deepens. Anger builds. Relationships sour. Our wellbeing suffers.

If you stop to think about it, we live in conversations. The 'private conversations' in our heads. And the 'public conversations' we have with others.

Conversations form the lifeblood of our relationships (as shown in figure 5). They form the currency of influence in any relationship, family, community, team or organisation. It's why the quality of our relationships is determined by the quality of the conversations we have in them.

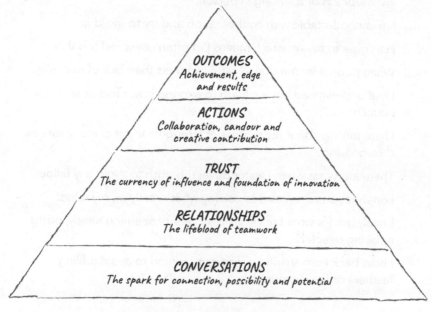

Figure 5: conversations count

THE MOST IMPORTANT CONVERSATIONS ARE OFTEN THE LEAST COMFORTABLE

Yet too often the conversations you most need to have are those you least want to have. For all the reasons cited above — too awkward, too uncomfortable, too risky. It feels easier, safer, to say nothing, at least in the short term which, let's face it, is what most of us are focused on.

So before we go any further, go through the list below and tick every line that applies to you 'at least some of the time'.

- ☐ I use email (or instant messaging, or text) to avoid the awkwardness of speaking in person.
- ☐ I'm uncomfortable with confrontation and try to avoid it.
- ☐ I struggle to say no which means I'm often stretched too thin.
- ☐ When people let me down I rarely address their lack of reliability.
- ☐ I feel undervalued but am loath to express how I feel or set clear boundaries.
- ☐ I hate talking about my success or strengths lest it come across as showboating.
- ☐ There are times when I water down the truth to avoid any fallout.
- ☐ I often resort to sarcasm to convey what's really on my mind.
- ☐ I rarely ask for what I really want for fear of seeming needy, pushy or being rejected.
- ☐ I hold back from sharing a different opinion to avoid ruffling feathers or feeling stupid.

How did you fare? Your innate instinct to avoid discomfort, combined with the pressures of your job (to have all the answers, get things right the first time, execute decrees from above) often sets the stage for playing it safe in conversations. But it's through your conversations that you're able to build relationships, grow influence, feel fully valued, and contribute more value to other people. In other words, it's through your conversations that you're able to fulfil your own potential and unlock potential in others as well.

The conversations that demand the greatest vulnerability are often those that hold the greatest potential — to inspire change, build trust, heal wounds, build bridges, expand possibilities, end conflict and wage peace. So if there is something you genuinely want to say, chances are someone genuinely needs to hear it.

Regardless of how cautious or timid you've been in your conversations until now, you have the ability to speak bravely and, in doing so, effect positive change — in your own life and in the lives of others — one courageous conversation at a time.

So no matter how much you've shied away from giving voice to your thoughts and feelings for fear of what might happen if you do, you have within you the ability to learn how to speak up about any issue with any person at any time.

Engaging in conversations about sensitive issues requires self-awareness, emotional intelligence and a solid dose of courage. Mustering up that courage takes getting real about the price you pay when you don't — the cost to your stress levels, your relationships, your influence and your ability to achieve what you want and change what you don't. If you're in a leadership role, this is amplified further.

After all, 'people are the project'. If you're not managing the people issues, you're destined to fall short on every other outcome. Research by VitalSmarts found a strong correlation between the span of time it took between a problem being identified and it being raised with team performance. Before the pandemic when most people went to the office every day, the average time was two weeks. It's likely to now be longer.

Over the course of life, there will be a multitude of courageous conversations that you need to have. None will be comfortable. All will contain some element of risk and invite you to be a little bolder and more daring than you have up until now. Or maybe a lot more. Here are seven conversations you need to dare to have. Start with mustering the courage to ask for what it is that you most want.

DARE TO ASK FOR WHAT YOU *REALLY* WANT

Ever find yourself feeling resentful, overwhelmed, underappreciated and wishing people would stop doing something you don't like, or start doing something you do or just make you feel more valued?

The reality is that other people will rarely care as much about our needs, preferences and desires as we do. And yet when our wants and needs aren't being met we often fail to make a request that would address it.

Maybe it's your boss who has unreasonable expectations, or a co-worker who's overstepped your boundaries. Perhaps you feel taken for granted by your partner. Whatever the case, feelings of overwhelm, frustration and resentment are generally the symptoms of a lack of requests. So if you have found yourself wrestling with any of those emotions, chances are there is a request that you need to make that you haven't been making (or you haven't been making effectively).

A client told me how frustrated she was with a colleague. I asked her if she'd been specific about what she wanted this person to do. 'No, they should just know,' she replied. And therein lay the problem. They did not know! So never assume people just know what you want or don't want. Even the people who know you best cannot always read your mind. Yet often we fall into the trap of assuming that they should 'just know' your innermost thoughts, wants and desires. Then when they don't act as you'd like, you get hurt and upset and lay all the blame on them.

> **For any relationship to thrive, all parties must take responsibility for clearly communicating their needs. No assuming. No hinting. No waiting for others to 'pick up' on your subtle innuendos. So decide your ideal outcome and then, standing tall in your worth, ask for it. Not in an entitled way. Not in an aggressive way. But in a way that conveys that you know your worth.**

Don't dilute your request to minimise the possibility of being turned down. Likewise, don't use hints in the hope that people will just 'get it' and make a change. Be specific about what you want and don't assume others share the same context as you. Asking someone to do something 'soon' can be interpreted in all sorts of ways. It's unreasonable to expect to get what you want if people aren't clear about what that is.

While you may not always get what you want (whether it be a pay rise or the corner office) you will nearly always end up with more than you would have received otherwise, had you not been bold in your request.

Take Jacinta, for example. A professor at a prestigious university, Jacinta had been working incredibly long hours and was feeling increasingly resentful about her salary. When I asked her if she'd communicated that to her boss she replied, 'I don't see the point. There's been huge funding cuts and the chance of getting it are slim to none.' I encouraged her to simply have a conversation with her direct supervisor to convey how she felt underpaid and was overdue an increase. 'What do you have to lose?' I argued. She promised she would.

My phone rang a week later. 'As I expected, I was told there's no funds for any increases,' she said, sounding disappointed but also pleased with herself for having actually raised the issue. Empowered by her own agency, she decided it was worth casting her net wider for opportunities outside her current university. Conversations ensued about other positions in the months that followed. However, before she had committed to another role her supervisor asked to meet. He'd received more funding and offered her a 15 per cent salary increase plus a large research grant beyond any she'd ever had before. She couldn't believe it and rang me excitedly: 'Champagne's on me next time.'

I took her up on that.

It's a rule of life that you get what you tolerate and you will rarely get more than what you're willing to ask for. By not risking a rejection, we reject ourselves before anyone else can.

Making requests will go a long way to eliminating the 'tolerations' in your life, whether it's asking a team member to show up on time or asking your colleague to stop making sexist jokes. Every day, through what you say and do, you teach others how to treat you. If you allow others to take you for granted, to overstep your personal boundaries, or to be outright disrespectful, you are complicit in it. Letting others know what you expect from them as well as what you will (and will not) tolerate is crucial to both your professional success and personal wellbeing.

So ask yourself, what are you no longer willing to tolerate? Therein lies the boundary that you alone must set and the requests you alone must make.

Of course, you won't always get what you ask for. At least not right away. Maybe never. Such is life. But at least now people know what you want, and you know where things stand. When that happens, don't over-personalise the response. The very act of taking responsibility for communicating what you want will reinforce your own sense of value and agency. So whatever you are 'tolerating' right now, dare to ask for what you really want. Who knows … you might just get it!

DARE TO DISAGREE

'Whatever your career, you have to be willing to take risks, to speak up and to push back when you don't agree with what others are thinking.' This was the advice Kathy Calvin, CEO of the United Nations Foundation, gave me as we discussed the importance of courage in any organisation and throughout her career.

Jim Rohn said, 'You don't get paid for the hour. You get paid for the value you bring to the hour.' When all you do is 'go along to get along', you deprive others of the value your perspective holds. Everyone is worse off.

You can push back without being 'pushy' in the traditional sense of the word. So be careful to distinguish that it's someone's opinion that you have an issue with, not them. Here are a few pointers to get you started.

Be armed with a recommended alternative solution.
It's easy to say 'I disagree'. So be sure you have another idea to offer. If appropriate, consider enlisting a 'co-conspirator' who is trusted by the person you're pushing back against.

Prepare ahead with good examples that support your case.
Since most people tend towards risk-aversion, demonstrating what others have done in similar situations can reduce their fear.

Ground your push-back or disagreement in a mutual concern or commercial basis.
Opinion is important, but if people see that there's a legitimate business reason that's driving your concern or disagreement, then it takes personal judgement and personality out of the equation and keeps the conversation focused on the content.

Move from advocating for your opinion to inquiring.
For instance, if there's something you disagree with say, 'I think I understand what you're trying to say but help me with this aspect: I'm having trouble seeing how to get from here to there'. By inquiring you're better placed to turn the conversation back to your winning points.

Instead of saying 'yes, but' say 'yes, and'.
The former negates anything that came before it and seems combative. The latter creates an extended conversation that builds on ideas already expressed and invites further conversation to expand perspectives.

If you realise you will not land your ideal outcome, let it go and move on. Graciously.
There's nothing to be gained by acting in ways that alienate yourself but a whole lot to be gained by showing up with the courage to speak up and the humility to move on.

In environments where 'yes men' are plentiful, experience has taught me that people respect those who have the courage to speak up and lay their reputation on the line for the common cause. Even more so when it's not a 'politically correct' opinion.

It's good to be nice. I'm all for kindness. However, if you say nothing when there's something you truly want to say for fear of hurting feelings or feeling awkward yourself, you are not serving those around you and are ultimately not being truly nice to anyone. Dare to speak your truth, with kindness and candour. Some may not like it, but better to be respected as a truth-teller than sidelined as insipid.

Will you be on this committee? Attend this panel? Meet for lunch? Give me an hour of your time … or three? Can I take you out for coffee and 'pick your brains'?

I like saying yes. At least in the moment I'm being asked. It gives me an immediate hit of people-pleasing gratification because I know it's what others want to hear and, well, I like making people happy.

But … I've learned that saying yes to something that takes away from more important things is not doing anyone any favours. Not them. Not me.

I'm sure you also have a lot of requests, offers and invitations coming your way. Some of them for things you'd genuinely like to do … if only you had more than 24 hours in the day.

The reality is that if you are someone who likes to make others feel valued and be a team player, then you probably sometimes struggle to say no and often wind up overcommitted to 'very good things' that you simply don't have time to do.

Let's face it: saying yes is easier than saying no in the moment we're being asked. But when you say yes for the wrong reasons — to keep people happy and avoid disappointing — you can ultimately end up disappointing yourself by short-changing yourself of the time you might otherwise spend on things that bring you an even deeper sense of fulfilment and wellbeing over the longer term. Saying 'yes' might spare you short-term discomfort as you see the disappointed look on someone's face, or just imagine as they read your email or listen to your voicemail. But if it will ultimately leave you stretched too thin or feeling resentful at the very person you've committed to — or yourself — you need to muster up your courage, and say no to the good so you can say yes to the great.

By the way ... you are great, going to bed early is great, not having every minute of every day scheduled is great ... so too is unscheduled time to just think.

DARE TO TOOT YOUR HORN AND PUT YOUR VALUE IN THE SPOTLIGHT

Growing up on a dairy farm, with six brothers and sisters, it was drummed into me from an early age that humility is a virtue, and bragging, well ... not so much. My parents, humble to the core, told us that if we worked hard and did a good job, we'd be recognised for our effort and rewarded accordingly.

For the most part, it was good advice. However, in today's competitive workplace, if your plan to get ahead assumes that hard work alone will suffice, you may find yourself being left behind as the horn blowers around you land the opportunities you assumed would be yours.

Research shows that people who are comfortable with promoting themselves are not only more successful in landing a job from an interview, but go on to build stronger networks — within their organisation and outside of it — and are more successful in business and throughout their careers. That's not to say that humility is no longer a virtue. But false humility can leave you languishing. Indeed, there's a distinct difference between tooting one's horn to stroke a needy or insecure ego (which is, after all, why braggarts brag) and sharing information that educates relevant people about who you are, the value you have to offer, and how you'd like to add more of it.

The old adage 'it's not what you know, but who you know' no longer holds true. Nowadays, it's 'who knows what you know'. Self-promotion is about strategically building your personal brand to ensure that those who can help you accomplish more in your career will know not just who you are, but the value you have (and want) to contribute. Letting fear of appearing conceited stop you from promoting yourself with the right people, in the right way, and at the right time doesn't serve anyone.

> Reframe self-promotion in such a way that it isn't about your 'self' at all, but about the value you have to give and would love to give more of. Share examples, not your ego. There's nothing as powerful as a well-told story to share a message without stating it directly, so there's nothing as powerful as an enthusiastically shared example of something you've done that conveys your accomplishments, capabilities and aspirations. We all gravitate toward passionate people.

Letting others know the value you can — and want — to bring isn't boastful or conceited. It's crucial. So stand tall in your unique value and humbly but confidently talk about yourself in ways that convey your belief in yourself and your passion to add more value in the future. Be willing to back yourself more and don't let your fear limit your future.

You have potential to fulfil and value to add — it's your responsibility to make sure those who can help open doors, make connections and create opportunities for you know what a talented human being and invaluable resource you are! So enough with false humility. Enough with playing safe and small. There are people (possibly even someone very close to where you are right now) who will benefit from knowing you better.

DARE TO STAND UP FOR YOURSELF

Lori Garver grew up in rural Michigan. After graduating with a Political Science degree she headed to Washington, DC, not sure what she would do with her degree but drawn to a career in the public service. 'I felt strongly that I wanted to make a difference,' she said. She had never set foot in Washington, DC, until the week after she graduated from college and turned up with no more than the phone number of someone she thought might be able to help her get a job, or even just a lead for a job.

After working on the short-lived presidential campaign of astronaut John Glenn, she landed an entry-level role at the National Space Institute as a receptionist-cum-secretary. Not one for inefficiency, she promptly set about streamlining her administration responsibilities, leaving her with extra time to initiate new programs and initiatives. She also went back to study at night to get her master's in Science Technology and Public Policy. Her initiative and 'can-do attitude' caught the attention of the board and, at age 27, after working at NSI for five years, she was asked to apply for the position of Executive Director. The man she'd been working under, who was in his 40s and with whom she'd shared an office, was actually in line for the role, but she was encouraged to go ahead and apply all the same. She got the job.

The morning she started in her new role as Executive Director, her previous supervisor left a note on her chair in their office saying that he would never work under her and expected equal pay. She asked him to come into her office and proceeded to fire him. He had been insubordinate, and she felt it was the only option if she was to perform well in her new job. He was stunned, as he never expected a 27-year-old 'girl' would fire him — particularly not on her first day on the job. Garver didn't do it to send a message, but it certainly communicated that she would not be someone others could push about. She was aware that we teach people how to treat us and was not willing to tolerate being treated with anything but the respect she deserved. It's a principle that has served her well.

In the male-dominated field of aerospace, Garver has been a trailblazer in her own right, combining motherhood and career as she paved new ground for other women in her field to eventually become the president of Women in Aerospace. Her willingness to stand her ground, challenge the status quo and trust in her ability ultimately led to her appointment by President Barack Obama as Deputy Administrator of NASA. She has since gone on to lead the Air Line Pilots Association and Earthrise Alliance.

DARE TO GIVE FEEDBACK THAT WILL HELP SOMEONE BETTER THEMSELVES

We all know it's important not to over-personalise critical feedback, but if you've ever received 'constructive feedback' you'll know that it's easier said than done, even when it's given in the gentlest of ways with the best of intentions. That's because hearing critical feedback strikes at the heart of two core human needs — the need to learn and grow, and the need to be accepted for who we are. Consequently, even a gentle suggestion to do something differently can leave us feeling wounded. Encouragement not to 'take it personally' often does little to soften the blow.

Yet just as you need to learn how to process critical feedback in ways that extract any value without permanently deflating your spirits, so too it's important to have the courage to give others feedback that would help them to learn and grow. Good for them; good for you; and if you're in a team or business, good for it too. In fact, research shows that organisations that provide regular feedback to employees have a 14.9 per cent lower turnover rate and are more competitive.

But let's face it: our fear of hurting someone's feelings or them reacting poorly often keeps us from sharing feedback. It's why before you do, you need to get crystal clear in your own head about why it's important for you to lay your own vulnerability on the line for the sake of the good your feedback might do.

Feedback should never be reactive, but given considerately, with the highest intention for the person you're giving it to. So before you open your mouth to offer feedback, take time to get clear about why you want to give it and how doing so will provide a genuine service to the person you're giving it to.

Likewise, criticism that comes from fear — or the fear-related emotions of insecurity, defensiveness, anxiety, anger, jealousy and pride — is guaranteed not to land well and will likely just amplify defensiveness. Sure, you may get something off your chest, vent your frustration and put someone back in their place, but at what cost to trust?

If you're unsure where or how to start, here's my simple ACED four-step framework to help you 'ace' it.

Ask for permission.
'Can I share some feedback with you that I hope will be helpful?' This simple question can reframe your words from being about you making a judgement to you trying to be helpful.

Current behaviour.
Be specific in describing the current behaviour you want to give feedback on.

Provide context by defining the *where* and *when* of the recent situation you're referring to.

Don't waffle on. Be clear, concise and come armed with recent examples to illustrate what you're talking about. For example, 'During this morning's meeting, when you gave your presentation ...'

Effect of behaviour.
Most people aren't aware of how they 'show up' for others.

Hearing that other people find you abrupt or unfocused, difficult or disorganised can feel like a punch in the gut.

So go gently in sharing the effect that you see someone's behaviour has on you and other people and how it might be confining their future success.

Make sure they understand why it's in their best interest to listen to your feedback and act on it accordingly. If they don't see how their behaviour is actually hurting them, it will be hard to motivate them to change it.

Desired behaviour.

Finally, state the behaviour you'd like to see more of. The more specific you can be, the better!

For example: 'When you cut me off in meetings (context and current behaviour), I feel undermined (effect on you). I also feel it comes across as abrasive to others (effect on others). In the future, I'd appreciate it if you let me finish what I'm saying before you share your opinion (desired behaviour).'

> **People may not always like what you have to say. They may not even agree with you. However, by not giving them the opportunity to hear what's on your mind — and how their behaviour impacts you, others and their own future — you're doing everyone a profound disservice. To quote behavioural scientist Dr William Schutz: 'If people in business told the truth, 80 to 90 per cent of their problems would disappear.'**

DARE TO HOLD PEOPLE ACCOUNTABLE

Perhaps you've been in a situation where someone didn't do what they said they would or did it too late or in such a way you had to do it yourself.

Of course, when faced with a pressing deadline, sometimes you have little choice but to do it yourself.

But time and time again, I've heard people complain about continually having to redo or improve on someone else's work because it wasn't done to their satisfaction.

When I ask them if they've addressed the issue with the person concerned, they often reply no. Sometimes they share that they didn't see any point in raising the issue. Most of the time they simply didn't want to go through the discomfort that such a conversation would entail. It was easier and less hassle to just do it themselves. But on nearly every occasion people's reasons for not holding someone accountable boiled down to fear of causing upset. It was just easier to ignore it. Easier, yes — courageous, no.

> Keep your word and hold others accountable to theirs. Nothing *demoralises* a great employee faster than watching the boss tolerate a lousy one. When you allow people to act in ways that dishonour core values and lack integrity, it undermines your own and pulls everyone down.

It's a general rule of thumb in life that you get what you tolerate. If you tolerate poor behaviour, you become complicit in your own misery. You teach people how to treat you, and teaching people that you're someone who expects commitments to be honoured will make a huge impact on what you — and any team you're part of — are capable of doing.

DARE TO TYPE LESS AND TALK MORE

Of course it's not just the conversations you need to brave that matters. It's how you have them that matters too. Should you send an email or pick up the phone ... or set up a video call?

A study published in the *Journal of Experimental Psychology* found that while people often err towards a text-based communication for fear of the awkwardness of talking in person, those with the courage to communicate verbally reap far better outcomes. The researchers found that verbal interactions forged stronger social bonds, yet (and here's the clincher) they were no more awkward than belting out an email or sending an instant message (IM). They also found that most people undervalue the positive impact on their relationships of verbal versus written communication.

So if you've been putting off having a brave conversation or you'd much rather put it in writing, take a moment to put yourself in the shoes of whoever you are talking to. In an era when we spend so much time on our devices, a real human-to-human verbal conversation — in which we can hear the tone of someone's voice and see their body language — can yield exponentially better outcomes, cultivate our interpersonal courage and forge far stronger bonds, all the while avoiding the potential pitfalls of written communications. Even using emojis to characterise emotion that could otherwise be conveyed with vocal intonation, subtle nuances, facial expressions and body language runs the risk of miscommunication, as people easily misconstrue what you meant. And the more sensitive the issue, the more prone people are to putting a negative spin on written words.

When it comes to building genuine relationships, quantity doesn't equal quality. Despite being more connected than ever, many people have never felt more alone. And those who report feeling most lonely are those you'd expect it from least: people under 35, who are the most prolific social networkers of all.

Technology makes it easier to stay in touch while keeping distance. The result: many people find themselves feeling increasingly distant and never touching. Or at least not enough. In today's overwired world, we humans crave emotional intimacy like never before. Yet genuine intimacy demands vulnerability and vulnerability requires laying down the digitally curated masks we can easily hide behind online, and revealing the raw truth of our lives.

So dare to talk more, text less ... and resist succumbing to the temptation to hide behind your screen and avoid the vulnerability of meaningful communication. No amount of speed typing can ever replace the value of simply talking.

You can spare yourself a lot of time and emotional churn in 'damage control' by taking the extra time up front to have a real conversation — whether on the phone, via video or in person. Doing so conveys you care and puts a big deposit of trust into your relational account. So whether you're addressing a behavioural issue, apologising for your own, or simply trying to influence an outcome, consider how you could be braver in not just what you say but how you communicate.

Email is an efficient tool for transactional communication, but it can be a very blunt one, if not outright counterproductive, for transformational communication in which emotions can run high. As a study by *Harvard Business Review* found, team performance went up 50 per cent when teams socialised more and limited email to only operational issues.

The price you pay for avoiding courageous conversations will always exceed their discomfort. So don't let your fear of what could go wrong keep you from speaking up to make things more right.

If there's something you genuinely want to say, chances are someone needs to hear it. Adopt the Buddhist principle of 'soft front, strong back' and stand firmly in your truth … coupling kindness with candour and courage.

Speak bravely.

5

LEARN, UNLEARN AND RELEARN

The thinking that got you here won't get you there

It is not the strongest of the species that survives, nor the most intelligent. It is the one that is the most adaptable to change.

CHARLES DARWIN

In 1946, Darryl F Zanuck, head of 20th Century Fox, said that 'Television won't be able to hold onto any market it captures after the first six months. People will soon get tired of staring at a plywood box every night'.

Sixty years later, when the iPhone was released in 2007, Microsoft CEO Steve Ballmer forecast that it wouldn't make a more than a dint in the mobile phone market. 'There's no chance that the iPhone is going to get any significant market share,' he predicted confidently. 'No chance.'

It's easy to laugh now at how wrong these men — highly respected business leaders of their time — were. However, if you didn't invest in Apple in the late 2000s, perhaps your thinking was also a little blinkered: unable to imagine how comprehensively Steve Jobs's new 'smart phone' technology would revolutionise our lives (or how Apple stocks would appreciate in the process!).

Zanuck and Ballmer did what many bright minds have done before them and you might also be doing right now — operating from a mental map comprised of assumptions that no longer hold true (or perhaps never did).

DON'T WALK INTO THE FUTURE BLINDFOLDED

To succeed in today's accelerated workplace and world, you have to be very deliberate in constantly challenging your own best thinking and open-minded about what's changing around you and how those changes — including the almost-imperceptible ones — will reshape the world five or 25 years from now. The more attentive you are to what's changing around you, the faster you'll be able to adapt to the challenges of tomorrow, and seize the opportunities that change always holds (though often obscured from clear view).

My kids have always struggled to comprehend how I ever managed any social life back in the Neanderthal pre–TikTok–Instagram–[*fill-in-the-blank-with-the-latest-thing*] era. Their 'digitally wired' brains boggle trying to imagine how anyone ever did their job without a digital device.

'We sent smoke signals,' I chide them.

In their digital world, as they video-chat with their friends on the other side of the earth, that may as well have been how we communicated. What they cannot yet appreciate is that by the time they are parents, their children will think the technology they're using today is as antiquated as the rotary-dial landline phone I relied upon not so long ago.

Adult-education experts estimate that up to 40 per cent of what tertiary students are learning will be obsolete a decade from now, when they will be working in jobs that have yet to be created. Indeed, the top ten most in-demand jobs today didn't even exist ten years ago. To say that we live in a changing world understates its pace and its vast scope.

Of course, it's not just technology that's changing the world. Consider the profound changes in demography and longevity, as well as the virtual workforce that was fast-tracked in the COVID-19 pandemic — coupled with the ongoing innovation in technology — and it's hard to imagine what the world and the workforce will look like 20 years from now. You can't do either by playing safe and resisting change. As *New York Times* columnist Thomas Friedman wrote, 'Standing still is deadly.'

When anyone can work from anywhere, it changes the nature of work everywhere. Traditional boundaries are disappearing, and the global talent pool is becoming more skilled and mobile, presenting challenges for people in developed countries to adapt faster in order to simply stay competitive.

There's no two ways about it: your ability to adapt to change will make a crucial difference to where you find yourself even just five years from now.

CHANGE BEFORE YOU HAVE TO

While my first 18 years of life growing up on a small dairy farm in rural Victoria, Australia, involved relatively little change, it's been constant ever since. Some of it I've eagerly pursued, albeit with moments of nervous apprehension. Some of it I've tripped through, awkwardly yet openly. And some of it I've struggled with, often overwhelmed and sometimes resentful. All of it I've grown from. Whether spending a year backpacking around the world with no more than a few nights in the same bed, having four children in five years across three countries in seven homes, or starting over with a new career in the middle of all those moves and babies, change is something I've become intimately acquainted with.

Needless to say, when it comes to adapting — to learning, unlearning and relearning — I've learned plenty by trial and error. As my husband and I support each other in pursuing our respective callings, and our children venture out into the world to explore and pursue theirs, I'm confident that plenty more learning awaits.

TREAT UNCERTAINTY AS THE NORM

We all want certainty and predictability, because our brains look for patterns. However, because life is the way it is, life can never stay the way it is. Whether in the form of a change of plans or a change of heart, change can be unsettling and uncomfortable. Just because you've made the choice to leave a job, relocate for a new job, take on a bigger role or transition into a new career — that doesn't mean it will, by default, be easy.

> You cannot become who you want to be by staying who you are. It is only by becoming comfortable with the inherent discomfort of change that you can find the hidden opportunities change always holds, and use them as a catalyst for the highest good, individually and collectively.

The more adept you are at initiating, navigating and managing change, the more successful you'll be in your job today and in the future. As social psychologist Daniel Spurk found in his research on adaptability in the workplace, employees who are adaptable are far more likely to leapfrog over those who aren't. The cost of rigidity and resistance grows steeper by the day. Sociologist Benjamin Barber wrote, 'I don't divide the world into the weak and the strong, or the successes and the failures … I divide the world into the learners and non-learners.'

CHANGE, EVEN CHANGE FOR THE BETTER, IS RARELY COMFORTABLE

How often have you heard people refer to 'the good old days'? It's generally not because life was any better ten or 30 years ago than it is now, but it reflects the affection most of us have for the past, and our innate aversion to what's new, untested, unfamiliar and unpredictable. When casting your mind back to days gone by, your selective recall filters out the anxiety and stress you felt in 'the good old days' and focuses instead on the happier memories, the irony being that you will one day look back on today as 'the good old days'. Why wait?

As difficult as change can sometimes be, we don't always fear it. Most people I know enjoy variety; many actively seek it. Even the most timid, change-averse people enjoy some semblance of it. We wear different outfits and mix up our wardrobe — even men who wear a dark suit and white shirt to work each day still change their tie. I've been known to rearrange the furniture in my living room for no other reason than I grew tired of its configuration. As the saying goes, 'a change is as good as a holiday', and often less pricey.

The reason why so many people enjoy variety in their personal lives yet struggle with change in the workplace boils down largely to control. We like to feel that we have some control over our circumstances, yet in our jobs we often feel anything but. Our lack of control over the variables and our uncertainty about what lies ahead can overwhelm us, triggering fear and anxiety.

> We like to make plans based on a future we can predict. When the terrain grows unfamiliar, hindering us from planning ahead with any confidence, it makes us feel anxious and uneasy. Intellectually understanding that uncertainty is part of life or why a change is good often does little to alleviate our anxiety. Emotions will trump logic every time. Unless you confront your emotions, embracing the discomfort of uncertainty and change, they will continue to fuel any residual resistance and rigidity.

HOW DOES FEAR FUEL YOUR RESISTANCE TO CHANGE?

Fear comes in many shapes and sizes. Often it disguises itself in excuses, procrastination, rationalisations and elaborate justifications for why 'now is just not the perfect time'. Yet the fears you don't own will own you.

Take a moment to reflect on where your own fears may be unconsciously keeping you stuck and holding you back from making a change or accepting one that is already headed your way.

- ☐ Fear of the unknown — What am I afraid might happen in the future?

- ☐ Fear of failure — Where am I afraid of falling short, messing up or being exposed as an imposter?

- ☐ Fear of success — What am I afraid will change if I achieve what I want? What extra challenges do I fear will accompany success?

- ☐ Fear of loss — What am I afraid of losing or missing out on?

REFRAME LEARNING FROM A ONE-OFF EVENT TO A LIFELONG JOURNEY

We're all born with the internal desire to learn. Babies stretch and grow their skills daily. Not just ordinary skills, but the most complex tasks possible: learning to walk and talk! Sure, their nimble brains are wired for it, but their egos have yet to develop and decide that the mistakes required to attain mastery are all too embarrassing for the effort. They walk, they fall, they get up. They just barge forward, bang their head, have a cry, then barge forward again. Likewise, you've probably seen children as young as two and three manoeuvring their way around their parents' iPhones with a speed and precision that leaves you feeling like the digital immigrant, born in a previous millennium, that you are. They just tinker with things until they've worked it out.

For children, free of pride and a need to preserve their public persona, the learning curve isn't something to be avoided or hastened, but rather to be travelled along until they have attained the mastery they want.

Somewhere along the line, though, many of us lose our love of learning. The pressure to excel in school, with its emphasis on test scores, can rob the enjoyment from the process of learning itself. Whatever the reasons, once they have the basics covered, many people tend to stick with what they know and avoid situations or challenges where they may mess up or be forced to learn something new. So they create a safe, secure and comfortable (and confining) world for themselves. In it, they do their best to mould the changes going on around them — in people, events and the general environment — to fit with their current 'mental maps'. They may say they're open to change, but do their best to avoid it.

For a while, that strategy can work fairly well. What it doesn't do is set them up for adapting to a future that may well require an entirely new set of maps.

> **Thriving in today's world is less about being smart or scoring high, but how quickly you can unlearn what you think you know and relearn what you need to know. Learning agility is the name of the game. If you're not engaged in a continual cycle of unlearning and relearning, you risk losing your place in a world that's marching steadily forward.**

LIFE WILL NEVER STOP TEACHING SO YOU MUST NEVER STOP LEARNING

Your smartphone holds more computing power than the entire mission control that landed men on the moon. At your fingertips is access to more knowledge than the entire Great Library of Alexandria, or all the books in the world just 100 years ago. So you could spend your lifetime trying to learn all the knowledge available to you and you'd only scratch the surface.

But let's face it, knowledge alone is of little value if it cannot be meaningfully applied in the world in ways that contribute value.

Getting ahead today requires lifelong learning, and that includes unlearning the old rules and relearning new ones. It requires emptying the melting pot of assumptions about how things work, 'unlearning' what you already know and making space to 'relearn' whatever is truly relevant in your job, your industry, your career and your life.

Learning agility is the name of the game. And in the game of life, where the rules are changing fast, your ability to be agile in letting go of old rules and learning new ones is increasingly important. Learning agility is the key to unlocking your change proficiency and succeeding in an uncertain, unpredictable and constantly evolving environment, personally and professionally. You may have to unlearn countless things in your job, business and career, even in the course of the next 12 months:

Unlearn how you collaborate with your team.

Unlearn the processes and systems you use.

Unlearn the technology you use or how you use it.

Unlearn how you communicate your brand and value.

Unlearn your target market, what they want and how they buy it.

Unlearning is about moving away from something — letting go — rather than acquiring. Indian philosopher Jiddu Krishnamurti believed that 'truth is a pathless land' and devoted much of his life to freeing his followers from their conditioned responses. Likewise, the process of unlearning is about liberation or freedom from what we *think* we know. It's a bit like scraping the old paint off a wall before you apply a fresh colour. If you haven't stripped back the old paint, the new layer can't stick. Unlearning, like stripping old paint, lays the foundation for the new layer of fresh learning to be acquired and to stick. But as any painter will tell you, stripping the paint is 70 per cent of the work, while repainting is only 30 per cent.

> **The key to learning, unlearning and relearning doesn't lie with the teacher. It lies with the student, with you: in your openness to being challenged and to letting go of knowledge that the passage of time has rendered obsolete (however hard you studied or worked to acquire it!). Likewise, in this book there will be ideas that ring true and concepts that resonate. There will also be some that don't (at least not yet). That's okay. You don't have to agree with, much less retain, everything you read here or anywhere. Nor should you. Whatever you get from it will be exactly what you need for where you are right now.**

QUESTION YOUR ANSWERS

Take a moment to amuse yourself with these statements. Imagine the lens through which those who made them viewed the world:

'*Sensible and responsible women do not want to vote.*'
Grover Cleveland, US President, 1905

'*There is no likelihood man can ever tap the power of the atom.*'
Robert Millikan, Nobel laureate (Physics), 1923

'*The Internet will soon go spectacularly supernova and in 1996 catastrophically collapse.*'
Robert Metcalfe, inventor of Ethernet, 1995

Needless to say, time has proven all of these people wrong. But had you lived at the same time, or even been an expert yourself in the same field as these people, you probably would have viewed the world through a similar lens and agreed with them. Many did. Their statements were, after all, the consensus opinion of many of the most brilliant minds of their time — minds likely no less brilliant than yours and very likely more brilliant than mine. And yet we know now that the things they held as 'the truth' were invalid assumptions based on limited and inaccurate information.

According to *Cambridge Advanced Learner's Dictionary*, an assumption is 'something you accept as true without question or proof'. As you read this, you have countless assumptions running in your life. Many of them serve you, and most likely at least a few of them don't. Unchallenged assumptions can limit you because where you're coming from often predetermines where you end up. That is, the assumptions that are guiding your choices today will impact where you find yourself in the future. It's possible one day you'll look back and wish you'd challenged some of them more vigorously. Common limiting assumptions I often hear:

'The first to market wins.'
Nope. Rarely. Google was the 22nd search engine.

'You can't do it if somebody else is already doing it.'
Again, not true. You just have to do it differently.

'I'm too young to ...'
Melanie Perkins was 19 when she came up with the idea for Canva ... she was a billionaire at 30.

'I'm too old to ...'
Leo Goodwin was 50 when he founded the Government Employees Insurance Company, now known as GEIKO. Colonel Sanders was 62 when he franchised his secret recipe for Kentucky Fried Chicken and Sister Madonna Buder, a Catholic nun, started running at 48 and went

on to become the oldest woman to ever finish an Ironman at 82 years old in 2012.

'You can't be a good mother and have a career ...'
That last statement I once made myself. In fact, I remember when my husband and I were considering having a fourth child. With three young children, I was aware of just how demanding parenting young children can be. I recall a conversation with my sister where I shared how, as much as I'd like to have a fourth child, it just wouldn't be possible to do that and start a new career in coaching.

'I just can't see how I can do both,' I remember saying. Fortunately, I married a supportive man who has always been my greatest champion and have some wonderful friends who cared enough for me to push back on that limiting assumption. My friend Janet said, 'Sure you can. I have a girlfriend who has four kids and runs a car dealership. You're every bit as capable as she is.' Another friend told me about her obstetrician, who also had four children while working in a demanding profession. Hearing about these women helped me realise that what I'd assumed to be true simply wasn't. Not only did I need to let go of the assumption that I couldn't do it, but I needed to let go of my ideas on *how* I would do it — by getting more help, doing much of my shopping online (which was far less common at the time than it is now), getting up earlier (which meant dropping the story that I was not a 'morning person'), stocking up on kids' birthday gifts and generally running my home more efficiently as well as accepting that 'good enough is often good enough'.

Like the queen in *Alice's Adventures in Wonderland* who thought of impossible things for half an hour each day, you want to train your mind to be more open to ideas that, at first, seem impractical, impossible or outright absurd. If you think of a hundred stupid, impossible ideas but one of them works, then consider it time well spent! When nothing is sure, everything becomes possible. To quote Alan Alda, 'Your assumptions are your windows on the world. Scrub them off every once in a while, or the light won't come in.'

Whenever Thomas Edison interviewed a job applicant, he would take them to lunch, where he ordered them a bowl of soup. Then, as he asked them questions about why they would be the best candidate for the job, he would pay attention to whether they seasoned their soup before tasting it. If they did, he would not hire them. He believed that if they had to season their soup before even tasting it, they were operating from so many built-in assumptions about everyday life that it would take far too long to train ('untrain' and 'retrain') them to approach their job with the level of creativity he felt they needed to be successful.

Edison's invention of a practical way of lighting, involving wiring circuits in parallel and then using high-resistance filaments in light bulbs, had never been considered by anyone else. It wasn't that others had assumed it wouldn't work; they just hadn't ever thought of it. But because Edison refused to work with any assumptions, he wasn't constrained in anything he did. The result: you have light bulbs throughout your home right now as you read this!

We human beings are assumption-making machines — we make assumptions on a daily basis. Doing so helps us to function effectively. The problem arises when we delude ourselves into thinking our assumptions are 'the truth'. When you reverse your assumptions you're forced to look for ways to explain the opposite of what you've perceived to be true. Even if you ultimately can't agree that the opposite of your assumption is valid, it can still shift how you were seeing things.

Management guru Peter Drucker advocates for recognising the value of ignorance: 'You must frequently approach problems with your ignorance; not what you think you know from past experience, because not infrequently, what you think you know is wrong.'

German psychologist Erich Fromm wrote: 'Creativity requires the courage to let go of certainties.' It's why, when facilitating leadership teams, I often ask them to list and then reverse their assumptions, just to generate creative thinking. Being forced to approach something from a different angle often generates a level of creative thinking that ultimately leads to other ideas. These ideas can often be applied to solve problems and be more innovative in other parts of a business.

VU DÉJÀ: SEE THE OLD WITH NEW EYES

Have you ever had that strange déjà vu feeling where you find yourself in a situation and you could swear you've been there before, except you know you haven't? It's just not possible. Well the opposite of déjà vu — looking at an unfamiliar situation and feeling you've seen it before — is 'vu déjà' (a clever term originally coined by author Josh Linker) — looking at a familiar situation as if you've never seen it before.

Which isn't easy to do. That's because your brain is hardwired to play tricks on you. As any neurologist would tell you, your brain has been uploaded with special 'pattern recognition' software that has it constantly scanning your environment and matching any patterns it sees with ones that are stored away in your memory bank. For the most part, this is a good thing because it enables you to function efficiently: every time you see a stop sign you don't even have to read it to know that you have to stop your car before proceeding further. When you see something, your first instinct is therefore to conclude that a pattern is the same as one you've seen before, which leads you to react the same way as you have before. The problem is that often this isn't the case, particularly when the environment you're operating in is changing rapidly.

For example, trying to sell a product or service to a customer the same way you did in the past may not produce the outcome you want in the future. Even when things are still managing to produce a satisfactory outcome, it still pays to look at a situation or problem with a fresh set of eyes. Philosopher Bertrand Russell wrote, 'It's a healthy thing now and then to hang a question mark on things you have long taken for granted.'

In the 1980s, NASA challenged aerospace company Lockheed Martin to cut several thousand kilograms from a fuel tank that formed the structural backbone of the space shuttle. The effort stalled at the last 360 kilograms. As the blue-ribbon engineering team turned its attention to increasingly complex materials, one of the most junior line-workers suggested simply not painting the tank as a way to shed the extra weight. His idea was dismissed as far too simple. After failing to come up with another solution they circled back to it. It turned out that the 760 litres of white paint that was to be used to cover the tank would have added close to 360 kilograms to a device whose functional lifespan was about eight minutes and whose fate was to rest at the bottom of the Indian Ocean. Such is the power of looking at a problem with new eyes, unburdened by old assumptions.

> **The best way to think outside the box is to listen to someone who lives outside the box. People often discuss important ideas with the same inner circle of colleagues, but in doing that you can miss obvious answers. Someone with less expertise and 'inside knowledge' than you may see beyond others' unquestioned assumptions right away.**

As you read this now, think of a challenge or opportunity you're facing. Now imagine you were approaching it as each of the following people might and see what different perspective, insights and solutions occur to you.

You're someone you have always admired as being really wise, strategically brilliant or insightful about the things you care about (for example Oprah Winfrey, Warren Buffett, or your favourite author). How do you see it now?

You're Doc from Back to the Future *and you're 30 years in the future looking at this situation as it is today. How do you see it?*

You are a [choose a profession different from your own: builder, pilot, designer, banker]. What do you notice differently?

MAKE BIG PLANS, BUT USE A PENCIL

When it comes to adapting to change and finding the opportunity it holds, 'blessed are the flexible for they shall not get bent out of shape'. The ancient Chinese text of the *Tao Te Ching* says, 'Whatever is flexible and flowing will tend to grow.'

Professor EJ Masicampo at Florida State University conducted a study that demonstrated the importance of flexibility in achieving goals amid changing circumstances. He essentially broke his subjects — a group of 98 students — into two groups. One group was given a firm plan to achieve a specific goal of researching information online. The other group had the same goal but wasn't given any plan to follow.

Within the 'plan' and 'no-plan' groups, half of the individuals were given ample time to complete the task, while the other half had their time cut short. The 'plan' group with ample time was 95.5 per cent successful in finding the information they needed, well ahead of the 'no-plan' group (68 per cent). However, the 'no-plan' group's success rate (71.4 per cent) far out-rated the 'plan' group's (36.7 per cent) when they were both given a warning that they would have to complete the task early. When the 'no-plan' group was informed their time was to be cut short, they quickly adjusted what they were doing to find the information they needed, whereas those in the 'plan' group resisted deviating from their plan and were consequently far less successful.

When you choose to go with the flow of change, you free yourself from being whirled around like leaves on a blustery autumn day. It enables you to choose the actions you'll take, or not take, the conversations you'll have, the requests you'll make and where you'll focus your energy from moment to moment. It also enables you to be that much more flexible in how you respond. Because you're not stuck in any fixed pattern of behaviour, you're not glued to any particular plan of action. You're a free agent, untethered and ready to adjust your sails to optimise your situation and to make the most of the prevailing tide and winds.

While having a plan can help you be more successful in achieving a goal, sticking to it rigidly can work against you. The better approach is to create what I call a 'flexi-plan' that you're open to changing as you get new information and circumstances change.

So go ahead: make your plans, set your strategies, get into action, but be flexible and adaptable as you go along. Rigidity can be lethal.

DISRUPT YOUR DEFAULT RESPONSE

Try crossing your arms right now. Go on, put down this book and do it. Then try crossing them the opposite way. Harder than you thought, isn't it? We're all wired with automatic reflexes, responses and decision-making strategies when faced with seemingly familiar information or stimuli. This enables us to be more efficient. However, you can become too reliant on the same default ways of responding. In any area of life, the greater the number of ways you can respond to a situation, challenge, problem, person or opportunity, the more success-ful you will be.

> If you always respond the same way, you won't always respond the best way. The greater your repertoire of approaches to the challenges you face, the better the outcomes you'll achieve.

Responding with flexibility and agility in our rapidly changing world requires an ongoing trade-off between your naturally preferred way of responding to a challenge and a way that isn't as natural and easy for you. For every strength you possess, there's an opposite strength or trait that balances it out.

> Mental and emotional flexibility are crucial to changeability. Be willing to disrupt your default response, even if it feels awkward (and it probably will).

Reading through the list below, take note of the way you tend to respond to the changes and challenges in your life. What is your default preference? Consider how responding with its opposite may, on occasion, be more helpful to you, enabling you to be far more effective in achieving the result you want.

sensitive — tough

initiating — following

forceful — gentle

cautious — bold

task oriented — relationship oriented

structured — unstructured

outgoing — introspective

planned — spontaneous

compliant — noncompliant

serious — playful

creative — analytical

One way of approaching things may have generally worked for you in the past, but that doesn't mean it will work for you now. Responding well to change requires pulling from the full spectrum of emotional and mental alternatives.

The world's top tennis players have developed mastery across the various tennis strokes. Not only must they serve brilliantly, but they must also slice, smash, lob and volley masterfully. Sure, they each still have their favourite shots, those they can execute better than any other player — Serena

Williams's power serve or Roger Federer's one-handed backhand, for instance — but they know that a brilliant backhand or a killer serve isn't enough. To be competitive against their top-ranked opponents, they have to be strong across the board. The same applies for other competitive sports. After winning the 1997 Masters Tournament by an unprecedented 12 strokes, Tiger Woods set out to further finetune his golf swing so that he could achieve even greater success. As good as he was, he knew he could be better if he strengthened his golf swing.

As Anne Morrow Lindbergh wrote, 'Only in growth, reform and change, paradoxically enough, is true security to be found.'

Look at the most successful people you know and you'll notice that when it comes to change, they have the greatest number of different options available to them for responding. They know that to successfully navigate the twists and turns of life they must be agile and willing to approach things in different ways, depending on the circumstances; responding in the same way to something again and again will eventually cause grief and fail to produce the desired result.

So, if you're feeling some grief right now, while it's comfortable to approach your challenges in the same way as you have done many times in the past, consider how approaching it in a different (albeit less comfortable and familiar) way may produce a better outcome.

CHANGE IMPOSED IS CHANGE OPPOSED

For reasons that have never been clear, 65 million years ago dinosaurs suddenly disappeared after more than 165 million years on the planet. Palaeontologists have debated the cause of the dinosaurs' extinction, but high on the list of hypotheses is their failure to adapt to rapidly changing climatic conditions — particularly temperature. If a failure to adapt was the dinosaurs' Achilles heel, then the dinosaur is not alone in the history of evolution.

In his book *The Living Company*, Arie de Geus wrote, 'In the future, an organisation's ability to learn faster than its competitors may be its only sustainable competitive advantage.' Today's pace of change in business conditions may or may not be unprecedented, but it is surely spectacular and likely to accelerate from here. Like most things in business, rapid change is a double-edged sword: a threat but also an opportunity. Adapt to rapid change better than your competitors and you can make great strides; ignore rapidly changing circumstances and expect to go the way of the slide rule, horse and buggy, wind-up watch or dinosaur. Adapting may be difficult, but it's not impossible.

Organisations, large and small, that are most likely to be successful in leveraging change — internal and external — to their advantage are the ones that no longer view change as a discrete event to be managed, but as a constant opportunity to evolve, iterate and upgrade their offering.

Adapting to our ever-changing world requires a fundamental shift in how you approach learning, and a willingness to be okay with 'not knowing'.

> **Change readiness has replaced change management. Learning, unlearning and relearning must not be regarded as a means to an end but as an end in itself — one that's fundamental to your ability as an individual, and collectively in the organisation, to remain relevant to all stakeholders.**

ACT OR BE ACTED UPON — KEEP UPGRADING YOUR SKILLS

While it's important to be flexible and 'go with the flow', it's just as important not to be complacent. Assuming that the skills and knowledge that got you to where you are today will get you to where you want to be five years from now could be a career-limiting mistake.

> **Thriving in today's accelerated age requires shifting from being a knowledge expert to becoming a knowledge entrepreneur. Develop the learning agility required to quickly unlearn what you *think* you know so you can relearn what you *need* to know.**

New York Times columnist Tom Friedman wrote, 'Everyone has to bring something extra; being average is no longer enough. Everyone is looking for employees who can do critical thinking and problem solving … just to get an interview. What they are really looking for are people who can invent, re-invent and re-engineer their jobs while doing them.'

LOOK WHERE THE PUCK IS GOING

When asked about his success, ice-hockey star Wayne Gretzky explained, 'I skate to where the puck is going to be, not where it has been.' Of course the challenge is to know where the hockey puck is going to be! There are opportunities in the future that we can't quite imagine yet, but by looking around our immediate environment and taking note of the problems people are dealing with and the changes in the way we do things, we can start to anticipate where there will be future needs and problems that are yet to fully emerge.

Similarly, the jobs of the future have not yet been imagined, much less created or had job descriptions written for them. Look for cracks in the infrastructure of your company and industry. What are they doing that they could be doing better? What problems are there that need fixing? Given the way things are changing, what problems are likely to arise in the future? How can you find solutions to the problems?

The opportunity in today's job market is that you have greater latitude to write your own job description and shape a role for yourself simply by being proactive, spotting problems that need to be fixed, anticipating future needs and taking the initiative to come up with more creative ways of filling them. As I've told my kids many times, be tenacious!

Change, wanted or not, is the only constant you can truly rely upon. And change, wanted or not, is something you must learn to navigate, adapt to and embrace if you're to not just survive but thrive in your career and life. But set realistic expectations: if you find yourself dealing with change, whether it be change you initiated (moving into a new career), change you were hoping for (landing yourself a promotion) or change that was thrust upon you (being told you no longer have your job or being assigned to a role you would never have chosen), don't be hard on yourself when you find yourself feeling less than robust.

As I've learned myself over the years — most recently moving back to the US after nine years living in Australia and Singapore — when your world tilts off its axis it tends to throw you off balance, at least for a while. When it does, heed the words of Albert Einstein:

'Life is like riding a bicycle. To keep your balance, you must keep moving.'

6

EMBRACE SETBACKS

Transform adversity to rise to higher ground

Nothing in life is to be feared, it is only to be understood. Now is the time to understand more, so that we may fear less.

MARIE CURIE

I know you have problems. Me too. Some small and mundane. Others daunting and less easily solvable. Perhaps not solvable at all.

Yet mastery of life is not the *absence* of problems. It is the *mastery* of problems. Solvable and not. If you look back on your life to date you'll see that it was the times you had the biggest problems that you learned the most, grew the most and discovered strengths that may otherwise have lain dormant. As Winston Churchill once said, 'Kites rise against the wind, not with it.'

Learning to reframe your problems through a larger lens will liberate you to live with less angst, lead better under pressure, to rise stronger and to blossom into the biggest, bravest person you have it within you to become.

Those people who forge deeply meaningful lives that leave the world better off are not those who've just 'got lucky' or were spared the streams of daily problems that befall the masses. Far from it. They are those who've learned to live from a place of self-trust, grounded in their capacity for life and committed to making the very best of whatever life brings their way (as illustrated in figure 6).

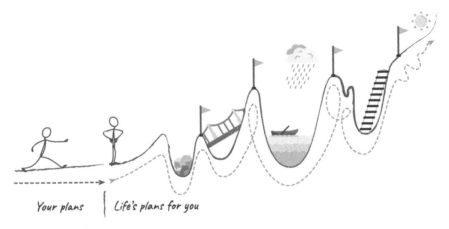

Your plans | Life's plans for you

Figure 6: life's reality

This not only spares them enormous stress, but emboldens them to pursue more meaningful endeavours that ultimately invite more problems into their lives. If you think about the most successful people you know you'll realise that they actively pursue challenges that only land more problems on their plate.

So imagine the energy and courage you would unleash in your life right now if you could trust yourself that whatever happened, however things turned out, you could handle it and find good within it. (Building self-trust is the focus of my book *You've Got This!*). Consider how operating from that mindset would transform how you approach your career, your relationships and your life overall.

What goals would you take on that you've shied away from?

Where might it fuel your ambition to pursue something bigger?

How would it empower you to make a change you've procrastinated about?

How would it embolden you to move boldly towards the highest vision for your future?

The ancient-Greek mathematician Archimedes said, 'Give me a lever long enough and a fulcrum on which to place it, and I shall move the world.' Likewise, when you build resilience you extend the length of your psychological lever, turning the setbacks that can weigh you down into stepping stones that advance you forward.

Building agility and resilience is the name of the game when it comes to leveraging your obstacles into opportunities in a pressure-laden world. In today's competitive workplace, resilient people not only take on bigger challenges and handle them better, but they think more clearly when they find themselves in a crisis and find opportunity amid the uncertainty.

> **Aspiring to a life free of challenges is asking for a life devoid of fulfilment. Studies in positive psychology have found that people flourish most when they are actively working towards meaningful goals that stretch them, not when they avoid hard things or try to minimise stress in their lives.**

You come to forge your sense of self and experience life at its richest in the process of learning how to rise above your struggles and do hard things. The good news is that you have everything it takes to do just that.

BUILD YOUR MUSCLES FOR LIFE

Building resilience and emotional mastery is one of the few things that improve with age. Research into brain plasticity has proven that human beings have an innate ability to build 'emotional toughness' until the end of their lives. This means no matter how well (or abysmally) you may have responded to your past challenges, you can learn to respond better in the future.

A modern understanding of resilience has its roots in the research of Salvatore R Maddi. In the mid-1970s, Maddi began a 12-year project to evaluate the psychological wellbeing of managers in a telephone company. The study took an unexpected turn six years later when the government deregulated the telephone industry. Half of the employees were laid off. For two-thirds of this group, the transition was traumatic — many were unable to cope and died of heart attacks or strokes, engaged in violence, got divorced or suffered from poor mental health. But the other third didn't fall apart, despite having been dealt the same hand of cards. Their lives actually improved. Their careers took off on new paths, their health improved, and their relationships blossomed. 'At the time the general idea was that you should stay away from stress,' Maddi recalled, 'but it turned out that some people thrive on it.' Maddi found that what distinguished the one-third who emerged from their job loss better off than everyone else was a shared characteristic he called 'hardiness'.

In essence, hardy people have learned how to respond to their challenges with greater resilience. They make a conscious choice to treat their crises (aka problems, pressures, challenges, failures, disappointments, mistakes and setbacks) as opportunities. Maddi believed that hardiness is the key to finding the courage and motivation to do the hard work of growing and developing rather than denying and avoiding. Numerous other clinical studies since have supported Maddi's belief that, with conscious effort, we can improve our ability to cope with stress and handle adversity.

However safe people play it, we all arrive at points throughout our lives where our plans collide head-on with reality, often in ways that we never predicted, much less planned for. Right now there are millions of people out of work around the world — and not by choice. Of those who do have a job, 70 per cent report that their work causes them to feel stressed or anxious on a daily basis. Potentially destructive emotions such as rejection, failure, shame, embarrassment, disappointment, anxiety, resentment, anger and hurt rise to the fore as they struggle to cope with competing commitments, make plans based on an uncertain future, manage unrealistic expectations, try to adapt to evolving market forces, and deal with myriads of challenging people and circumstances on a daily, often hourly, basis. Little wonder stress is the number-one cause for visits to the doctor's office.

BEWARE NEGATIVE FORECASTING BIAS: YOUR TENDENCY TO TURN FORECASTS INTO FEAR-CASTS

Daniel Gilbert, a Harvard University psychologist, said people are generally not good at forecasting their feelings when they're in the midst of a period of crisis. When feeling overwhelmed with negative emotions, they wrongly assume they will feel similarly in the future. Gilbert speculates that this negative forecasting bias developed because it's useful, serving to overestimate risks and steer people away from dangers. But, he argues, this also means they tend to underestimate their capacity to recover: 'It's not that things don't hurt. It's that they don't hurt quite as long or as much as we think they're going to.' It's why crises tend to drive people to play safe and make short-sighted decisions that work against their best interests in the longer term. This helps to explain why someone I know decided to cash in their entire retirement savings at the start of the COVID-19 pandemic. As fear of an Armageddon-like disaster loomed large in their imagination, they overreacted to shore up short-term security ... ultimately paying a hefty financial price.

By expanding your capacity to cope with your pressures and problems, you can curb the tendency to turn forecasts into fear-casts and expand your capacity for finding opportunity amid adversity. To help you do that, I've developed the following simple five-step framework.

PREPARE TO SOAR: LIFE DOESN'T HAPPEN *TO* YOU, BUT *FOR* YOU

Drawing from a combination of neuroscience research, mindfulness and emotional intelligence, the SOAR process (shown in figure 7) will help you to soar above life's stressors, which might otherwise pull you down and sabotage both your happiness and success.

> History shows that all stories of success are also stories of great failure. Just as smooth seas don't make skilful sailors, neither does a boom economy or challenge-free environment make for a high-performing employee or, for that matter, an innovative, leading-edge company. You acquire insights and find smarter, more creative ways of thriving in the future through the process of rising up to meet your challenges and bouncing back from your setbacks (aka 'stuff-ups').

Committing each of the four steps of the SOAR process to memory will enable you to intervene in your instinctive response to threats, ward off 'neural hijack' and respond to your situation more confidently, calmly and constructively.

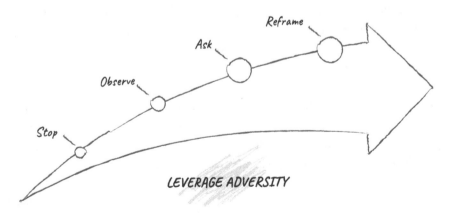

Figure 7: the SOAR process

STEP 1: STOP

Calm, focused people are far more effective than stressed-out people whose focus is scattered and patience is short. So the first step of the SOAR process — to simply cease your busy doing and take a 'sacred pause' — helps override the stress response so you regain your centre and clear your thinking. Amid the constant pressure to be 'doing', this is important!

In the 1997 world-heavyweight-boxing title match Mike Tyson became so enraged that he bit off a chunk of Evander Holyfield's ear. His momentary lapse in sanity cost him $3 million — the maximum penalty that could be taken from his $30 million winning purse — and a year's suspension from boxing. Tyson's aggression was the result of a 'neural hijack'.

While you may never have felt the desire to bite off a chunk of someone's ear, you've likely experienced your own version of a neural hijacking. Think of the emails you've sent off in a moment of anger. How did they work out for you? Or the way you've snapped something unkind in a moment of anger. Didn't go down too well, right? Road rage is another example — when a driver literally tries to kill their fellow motorist for cutting into the lane in front of them. An extreme example, perhaps, but I'm sure you've had plenty of up-close and personal encounters with neural hijacking that have caused you to react, or *over*react, disproportionately to a situation, producing a less-than-optimal result, if not an outright dreadful one.

The reason Tyson acted so foolishly — and why you might also have done some things in the heat of the moment that you later regretted — can be explained by the primitive emotional region of our brain called the autonomic nervous system (ANS), the 'kneejerk' part of the brain. About the size of a walnut, it constantly scans your environment for threats and danger. When it perceives a potential threat (generally triggered by a past traumatic experience), it signals to release the hormone cortisol, which is the body's response to stress. Cortisol floods in, mobilising you into action, to escape, protect, defend or change the situation — in other words, to cope. In the process, it overrides the cerebral cortex: the more logical, rational and 'thinking' part of your brain. You undergo a 'neural hijack' when the 'kneejerk' part of your brain overrides the 'thinking' part, driving you to react in a primitive, instinctive way. When your emotions hijack reason and logic as you react in an instinctive way to a perceived threat, the results are rarely helpful and often harmful.

> **The instinctive fight-flight-freeze alarm reaction that enabled our cave-dwelling ancestors to fight off predators on the African plains millennia ago can still help preserve our own lives when we're faced with a genuine life-or-death situation. But therein lies the problem: we rarely are. The same parts of our brain where we process threats to our life are triggered when we perceive the threat of financial loss or even loss of pride (social status). So reacting with alarm is a helpful thing, once in a while — a life-and-death while — but the rest of the time it can cloud your thinking and drive you to overestimate a risk and overreact destructively.**

Although you can't just turn off the turbocharged, kneejerk-reactive part of your brain, you can learn to manage it. It takes three to five seconds to re-engage the 'thinking' part of your brain. So stopping and taking a step back can help when you find yourself facing a situation that triggers your 'feel alarm' response. It gives your rational brain time to come online and infuse some logical thought into responding.

The simple act of stopping what you're doing and gifting yourself with a few long, deep breaths can make all the difference to your life. Mindful breathing brings you back from 'What if?' fear-casting to the present moment. Studies have found that even as little as 20 seconds of deep, mindful breathing can short-circuit the reactive fear response and help people respond with greater clarity and calm.

As you press the pause button amid your busyness, bring your attention to your breath. One of your body's natural responses to feelings of stress is to take shallower breaths. But shallow breaths leave your bloodstream (and your brain's central command centre) deprived of the full quota of oxygen it needs to keep performing at its peak. So as you pause what you're doing and step back from the fray, notice how much oxygen you're breathing down into your lungs and then proceed to take at least five long, slow, deep breaths. Just try it right now and observe the difference it makes even while you're in a relaxed state.

> To restore calm and bolster courage, take the deepest breath you have all day ... slowly ... then slowly breathe out again. Do it ten times, counting as you go. If for some reason you don't think you have two minutes to spare for this, take ten. Consciously deciding to stop what you're doing when you're mid-flight can be the most fruitful exercise you'll do all day.

STEP 2: OBSERVE

Wayne Dyer once wrote that when you change the way you look at things, the things you look at change. Neuroimaging studies have found that when people consider problems from the position of a detached observer, they use brain circuits additional to those involving simply problem-solving.

Curiosity is a valuable attribute when it comes to finding better ways of approaching problems, engaging with people around you and deciding the best path forward. Indeed, curiosity is one of the most common attributes found in healthy and happy people and one that's most often missing from those who are particularly anxious and depressed. People who suffer from depression are often absorbed in their own problems and show little curiosity about the world around them. Looking outwards on your situation interrupts the stream of negative thoughts.

On returning to Earth after his first journey into space, astronaut Neil Armstrong said, 'It suddenly struck me [in the space capsule] that that tiny pea, pretty and blue, was the Earth. I put up my thumb and shut one eye and my thumb blotted out the planet Earth. I didn't feel like a giant. I felt very, very small.' Nothing shifts our experience of life more profoundly than shifting the perspective from which we're viewing it.

Orville and Wilbur Wright didn't invent flight by focusing on the laws of gravitational pull. Nor did they succumb to the pressure to agree with the consensus opinion of the time — that it was mathematically and physically impossible to build a vehicle that could defy the laws of gravity, elevate and stay in the air for more than a moment. With little formal education but a lot of mechanical know-how gained from working in their bicycle-repair shop, the Wright brothers kept their focus firmly on building a vehicle that could defy the laws of gravity. Thank goodness they did!

You don't see the world as it is, but as you are.

Of the nearly 8 billion people on this planet, not one observes the world the same way as you do. Oh sure, there may be quite a few who see many things similarly to you. There may be many who have the same political views or religious beliefs or who follow the same parenting principles. But no-one sees everything exactly the same way as you do.

So after you've paused, taken a step back and breathed some precious oxygen back into your brain, don the hat of 'curious observer'. Visualise yourself soaring up to skyscraper level (lower if you're afraid of heights!) and look down on the situation you're currently struggling with. When you actively try to see things from a bird's-eye perspective, it expands the choices available to you for responding.

What do you see? As you look down, ask yourself how the way you've been observing things until now has caused you to feel anxious or upset. From your new, heightened perspective, consider how else you could be observing the situation. Where have you been overly focused on one aspect and failed to notice others? Consider how someone else — particularly someone whose opinion you respect — might observe it differently.

Try now to observe what you're thinking while being asked to observe what you're thinking. Do you think it sounds like an interesting idea, or are you cynical and writing it off as foolish nonsense ... or something else? What are you observing about yourself as you do that?

> William James said, 'The art of being wise is the art of knowing what to overlook.' So take a look at how you're looking at your life and whatever is causing you to feel any angst or upset right now. Observe the critical judgements that you make. Is your lens tinted with optimism or pessimism, excitement or anxiety, anticipation or dread, confidence or self-doubt? Notice how that lens shades your interpretation — of people, situations and yourself — and consider how those interpretations may be serving you and how they may be failing to serve you.

I once heard a story about a guy from a Fortune 500 company who made a $10-million error. Ashamed, he was readying himself to be marched out of the building when he was hauled up before the division president, who was known for his intolerance of those who failed to deliver. Pre-empting his dismissal, he apologised, then promptly offered his resignation. Refusing the resignation, the president said, 'Goodness, man, we can't lose you now! We've just spent $10 million on your education!'

> You are not determined by your experiences but you are self-determined by the meaning you give to them. That is, no experience is in itself a cause of success or failure. It's what you make of it that determines which it will be. How you see the problem is the problem.

Pioneering psychiatrist Alfred Adler, who founded the school of individual psychology, writes in his book *What Life Should Mean to You*: 'We determine ourselves by the meanings we ascribe to situations.'

When people attribute their failures to factors that can't be changed, adjusted or accommodated — whether internal or external — failure becomes a destructive and debilitating event. It leaves them feeling hopeless about the future, unworthy of success and unwilling to try again. In other words, people who interpret their failures and setbacks as being due to inadequate intelligence, a magnetic ability to attract bad luck or as evidence that they were born losers, are unlikely to go on to achieve much success in the same, or any, arena.

On the other hand, people who attribute their failures to a lack of knowledge that can be gained, poor systems that can be re-engineered, resources that can be acquired, strategies that can be reworked, timing that can be improved or even a shortfall in prudent judgement (which can be strengthened) are able to transform their failures into invaluable stepping stones. Indeed, the lessons their failures provide can be leveraged into priceless (and hard-earned) knowledge that truly can be the making, rather than the breaking, of their career, business, marriage or life.

> You can never be a failure, though you will sometimes fail to achieve what you set out to do. When this happens (as it inevitably will), remember: failure is not a person; it's an event. Avoid over-personalising or treating it as a permanent state. Rather, embrace its lessons and reframe it as a pre-requisite for progress.

Research by positive psychology leader Martin Seligman has found that it's how you explain your failures to yourself and others that determines your ultimate success. Seligman stated about his research, 'We discovered that people who don't give up have a habit of interpreting setbacks as temporary, local and changeable.' Often, we treat failure as a *permanent* state (I will always be a failure at public speaking), we generalise to all areas of our lives (treating it as *pervasive*) or we *personalise* it ('I'm such a loser for not getting that job'). Be vigilant for the three Ps.

Walt Disney spent his early years trying to make it as a cartoonist. He was rejected again and again while trying to get an entry-level job with newspapers. Several times he was told he lacked talent and should consider another career. But, fuelled by his passion, he didn't waver from his ambition to become a professional cartoonist or listen to those who didn't believe he could make a living creating storybook characters. He pressed on long after many would have given up. Eventually he achieved his first 'lucky break', in the form of a minister from a local church agreeing to hire him to draw some cartoons. So Disney went to work in a small shed near the church, which was infested with mice. He was inspired after seeing a small mouse, and the beloved Mickey Mouse was born. Disney later said, 'All my troubles and failures have strengthened me. You may not realise it when it happens, but a kick in the teeth may be the best thing in the world for you.'

While Disney's story is unique, it's also universal. The most successful people are also the most resilient; they are those who have had to scale career hurdles and bounce back from setbacks before achieving the success they've become known for.

> **Optimism enables you to succeed against the odds, not because you beat the odds, but because the odds didn't beat you. Life's challenges always have a way of working out in the end. If yours hasn't worked out yet, then you're not yet at the end. To quote the late Clive James, 'Stop worrying, nobody gets out of this world alive.'**

Life inflicts the same setbacks and tragedies on the optimist as it does on the pessimist. But, as Seligman wrote in *Learned Optimism*, 'the optimist weathers them better and emerges from them better off' — better off in terms of health, relationships, career prospects and finances. Psychologist Suzanne Segerstrom found that ten years after graduating, law students who were optimistic earned an average of $32667 more than their glass-half-empty peers. Another study at Harvard University found that those who choose to view their problems through an optimistic lens experience better health, including a lower rate of heart disease.

So not only is an optimistic lens good for your career, but it's also good for your health!

STEP 3: ASK BIGGER QUESTIONS

For much of the 1800s cotton was king in the American south, with millions dependent on it for their livelihood. Then, in the 1890s, the boll weevil — a beetle smaller than your pinky fingernail, which feeds on cotton buds and flowers — migrated across the border from Mexico and infested the cotton-growing areas. By the 1920s the industry was devastated and, with it, the people working in the southern states.

But rather than dwell on the crop they could no longer grow, people went to work finding out what they could grow, and began to plant alternative crops such as soybean and peanut. They also learned how to use their land to raise cattle, hogs and chickens. They discovered that, expanded from single-crop to diversified farming, their farms grew more prosperous. In fact, the people of Enterprise, Alabama, were ultimately so grateful for the boll weevil that they built a monument to it. The inscription read, 'In profound appreciation of the boll weevil and what it has done to herald prosperity.'

The disruption of the COVID-19 pandemic challenged companies to engage in 'creative disruption', elevating how they were viewing their problems to identify new opportunities hidden from obvious view. Shell Aviation is a case in point.

In May of 2020, global air passenger traffic was down by 91.3 per cent year-over-year with a devastating impact across the entire travel industry. Shell redirected resources to keep global supply chains functioning and transport medicines and medical equipment. They also seized the period of depressed demand for jet fuel to ramp up efforts to developing toward a 'net-zero' carbon world, collaborating across the industry with companies like Rolls-Royce, a leading manufacturer of aircraft engines, to improve sustainable aviation fuel (SAF) technology and increase its supply availability to customers like Amazon Air and DHL.

Forward-leaning companies like Shell ultimately used the cascading crisis of the COVID-19 pandemic to lead a global green recovery, finding better ways of fulfilling their purpose as a global leader in energy supply, serving their stakeholders, and all while bettering the world.

Often when things don't go as we want, we spend too much time focused on what interrupted our plans, and too little time asking questions to discover the opportunity contained in our challenges. In the case of the boll weevil, the farmers discovered that their assumed answers to the question, 'What is the best use of my land?' were wrong. The boll weevil drove them to consider the alternatives, which ultimately made them wealthier people.

> Growing up on a dairy farm I came to realise that the biggest problem about milking cows was that they never stayed milked. Likewise, you will never solve all your problems. And those you do solve will very quickly be replaced by others eager to take their turn in line. When we rail against our problems we rail against the fabric of life. It's only by choosing to view them from a different perspective that we can elevate ourselves above them, distinguish those we can solve from those we must accept, and then go about finding better solutions than those we've tried before.

When you don't like the results you're getting in life, it's probably because you're not asking the right questions. Nobel laureate Naguib Mahfouz said, 'You can tell a man is clever by his answers. You can tell he is wise by his questions.' Wise people don't assume they have all the answers. Rather, they ask questions to try to deepen their understanding of a situation or problem. Of course, you may not be able to find all the answers you're looking for, but by being willing to simply ask the questions, you will shift your perspective and you may find yourself coming up with answers you wouldn't have otherwise.

Our society places a lot of value on cleverness. But cleverness is not near as strong a predictor of success as curiosity, particularly when coupled with humility. A few years ago, when I had the opportunity to interview Bill Marriott, Chairman of Marriott hotels, he recounted a conversation he had with President Eisenhower as a boy. Eisenhower expressed how important it is never to assume you have all the answers and to be humble about what you think you do know. In recalling an executive in his business who valued his cleverness over humility or curiosity, Marriott said: 'If you think you're the smartest person in the room, pretty soon you'll be the only guy in the room.'

After spending time over the years with many clever people, I've come to learn that cleverness — as measured by IQ scores or even bank balances — has little to do with wisdom and even less to do with happiness. Many outwardly smart people have a marked absence of inner serenity. They're often full of answers to all but one question: 'So if I'm so darn smart, how come I'm unhappy?'

> As you think about your current 'problems' (or those 'problem people' you have to deal with), consider that your problems aren't 'out there', but that they're actually within you. Your problems are not the problem; it's how you view them that creates the problem. When you give up arguing against your problems and using your smartest answers to work them out, you can begin to ask better questions that can fundamentally shift how you see the problem itself. Your smartest answers landed you the problems you have today. Asking smarter questions confronts the reality you've constructed for yourself. Needless to say, that can be challenging. But what matters most is your willingness to sit with the questions.

Albert Einstein once said, 'Problems cannot be solved at the same level of thinking at which they were created.' When you ask bigger questions, you get better answers. Bigger questions serve to elevate and expand your level of thinking, which in turn enables you to take more effective actions to address your challenges, achieve your goals and make the most of your opportunities.

Think of a challenging situation or person you're dealing with right now. Here are some questions that could shift your perspective, the emotions you're feeling and the actions you'll take.

Not all questions will be relevant to your situation, but write down your answers to those that are. Remember, it's okay not to have all the answers. What matters most is that you're willing look at all the questions.

- [ ] How has my aversion to risk perpetuated this problem?
- [ ] Why have previous attempts to resolve this problem failed?
- [ ] What is my ideal outcome for this situation? What would need to occur to achieve it?
- [ ] What is it about this situation that I'm resisting? What would happen if I gave up that resistance?
- [ ] What is the fundamental underlying challenge for me here?
- [ ] How would someone I respect approach this?
- [ ] What emotions — fear, anger, jealousy, sadness, guilt — that could be undermining my response am I failing to fully acknowledge?
- [ ] Where am I focusing too much on some aspects of this situation and too little on others?
- [ ] What valuable lessons does this problem hold that I need to learn?
- [ ] What untested assumptions am I making that could be limiting my response?
- [ ] Where am I letting other people's opinions limit how I'm viewing this?
- [ ] Is there a pattern to this challenge or problem? If so, what is it?
- [ ] What is the single best thing I can do (or stop doing) right now?
- [ ] How can I apply the lessons I've learned from similar situations to deal better with this one?
- [ ] If I were to be courageous right now, what would I do?

STEP 4: REFRAME

Boats don't sink because of the water around them; they sink because of the water that gets into them. Likewise, you cannot always change the world around you, but you can always change the world within you. You can do that by reframing how you've been viewing your situation, and thus how you're experiencing it (calmly or like Tigger on Red Bull) and responding to it.

> **When confronted with a challenge, remember: you need to reframe your perspective, not your problem. There's a world of difference between a person who has big problems and a person who makes their problems big.**

When your car breaks down, your car doesn't have a problem. You do. The problem is yours because suddenly you find yourself stuck on the side of the road, or somewhere equally inconvenient, and unable to get to your intended destination. The same applies to whatever problems you're dealing with now. What you're viewing as the problem is really not the problem. The problem is the way it's impacting on you and your life. By seeing that your problems reside in you, you can step back and observe them from a fresh and heightened perspective and reframe them.

We experience stress according to how we assess our ability to meet a threat, real or perceived. In other words, a particular person, event or circumstance is not in itself 'stressful', but rather the assessment you make as to your ability to cope with that event. How you process or interpret that event (the 'stressor') gives rise to any feelings of anxiety or fear, which in turn produce a physiological change in your body (your heart beats faster, your palms sweat, and your breathing grows faster and shallower) and this in turn is what you label as stress. For example:

'I had a stressful day.'

'They're stressing me out.'

'I'm feeling stressed out.'

'My job is so stressful.'

The irony is that by talking about how much stress you feel, you create more stress. And as your stress goes up, your ability to engage the critical thinking part of your brain (where you come up with the best solutions to the problem at hand) goes down. In short: the more stressed you feel, the less smart you think.

Research shows that a certain amount of stress is good for you. It helps people achieve peak performance, whether in a sales presentation to a new client or preparing for an interview. Stress serves to focus you on what you're about to do and stress sharpens your focus. Harnessed well, stress helps you perform better and be more competitive, particularly when the stakes are high, the pressure acute and even the smallest competitive edge can make a difference.

Dr Hans Selye, who first coined the term 'stress' in the 1930s, warned an audience at a conference where he was asked how people could eliminate stress, 'If anyone tells you they can eliminate your stress, run. What they are really saying is that they want to kill you. The absence of stress is not health, it's death.' The reality is that stress is not a medical condition, but a psychological one that triggers physiological responses in the body.

> When horticulturalists are preparing their plants for life outside the hothouse, they gradually expose them to greater variations of temperature in order to toughen them up for the variability they will be exposed to in the natural environment. While we're more complex than plants, the same principle applies to us. Only by being exposed to situations that stretch you can you build your capacity, competence and courage for bigger challenges.

Conversely, without a period of strain you actually lose strength, endurance and natural resilience. Exposure to stress is the most important stimulus for growth. Without it, you wither on the vine of life. So think of stress as a valuable force of life that can be constructive or destructive, depending on how you manage it. Managed well, stress can be leveraged so that it will improve, rather than impair, your ability to live a fulfilling life.

Don't wish away all your stress. It's your stress that compels you to stretch, to grow and to perform at your best. You just have to keep it in check and learn to use it to hone your performance and sharpen your attention, not scatter it.

FOCUS ON WHAT YOU CAN DO, NOT WHAT YOU CAN'T

In 2008 my brother Frank was riding his motorbike across the large sand dunes outside Doha, Qatar, where he was working as an engineer. Frank was an experienced rider, having grown up riding motorbikes on our parents' farm, and always wore the best protective safety gear. On this particular ride, accompanied by two riding buddies, Frank went up a large sand dune that looked no different to any other. Unbeknown to him, over the peak was a sheer drop of about 10 metres onto a layer of solid rock. As Frank sailed through the air he wondered if he would be alive after hitting the rock. Fortunately he survived, but the impact shattered his T12 vertebra, leaving him paralysed from the waist down.

I arrived at the Doha Rehabilitation Hospital ten days after the accident. In the following days I spent a lot of time sitting beside Frank's hospital bed, where he was to stabilise for a few weeks before being flown back to Australia for full rehabilitation.

On the third day a specialist spinal-injury surgeon visiting from Sweden made his way through the spinal unit to visit the patients. When he arrived at Frank's bed he asked him how he was doing. Frank gave his usual cheerful reply, saying something about looking forward to walking into the ward one day to say hello to the nurses who had taken such great care of him. The elderly doctor looked at him kindly yet solemnly and said, 'Frank, I know this is very difficult for you to hear, but it is important for me to be honest with you. You will not be able to walk again. There is no cure for your injury. And so it is important for you to focus on your rehabilitation and on learning to live without the use of your legs. Your rehabilitation will not be able to help you walk again. But it will teach you how to live well within the limits of your injury.' It was a brutal moment. I still get a lump in my throat just recalling it.

> You may be shaped by your adversities, but you don't have to be defined by them. So don't wear your hardships or heartaches as your identity. Decide who you want to be. Never give an event the power to determine how you show up in the world. Your past does not equal your future, unless you live in it.

The next day I arrived at the hospital and talked to Frank about how he'd slept and what the latest estimate was on when he would be able to fly to Australia for rehab. He looked at me and said, 'Margie, can't say I much liked what that doctor said yesterday.'

'Nup. I get it, Frank. Who would, right?' I replied, tears welling in my eyes and my throat tightening.

'But you know,' he said reflectively, 'I'm not going to give this injury the power to keep me from living my life. There may be a thousand things I can no longer do, but there are still five thousand I can.'

It was life at its most poignant, raw, brutal and beautiful.

In that moment I witnessed courage I had never known my brother to have.

Talk about a reframe. I had never been so proud of Frank.

Countless times since then, I have felt the same pride overwhelm me as Frank reframed his circumstances and focused his attention on the many things he still can do. Last time we caught up at my home for our weekly Sunday-night roast, Frank had just returned from a scuba-diving holiday in Bali. The holiday before that he learned how to ski without the use of his legs. Next month he will be travelling overseas on business.

I've witnessed Frank respond with courage, resilience and good humour time and again. And I've pondered the many people with legs that work perfectly well, who confine themselves in mental prisons of their own making, feeling resentful of their circumstances and powerless to change them. This perspective on life prevents them from accepting what they cannot change and trying to change what they can.

As my friend Warwick Fairfax wrote in his book *Crucible Leadership*, which draws on his own experience of losing his family's 150-year-old business under his watch, 'When we embrace the crucible moments of our lives, we can leverage them to be our best selves. Understanding how we've been refined will help us understand who we truly are, so we can move forward and lead lives of impact and significance.'

Yale psychologist Charles A Morgan III studied naval personnel who undergo an intensive 12-day course that realistically simulates the experience of being captured and interrogated by an enemy force. Morgan found that people who embrace adversity as a natural part of living are less likely to exhibit symptoms that could grow into post-traumatic stress disorder (PTSD) and are more likely to experience what has been called posttraumatic growth.

> **Expecting that you'll sometimes have to confront new situations and deal with challenges that make you feel uncomfortable will enable you to respond versus react to all types of challenges — from the mundane to the significant. This applies as much to those circumstances you choose as to those thrust upon you.**

Psychologists Lawrence Calhoun and Richard Tedeschi coined the term 'posttraumatic growth' (PTG) to describe the phenomena whereby people emerge stronger in the aftermath of trauma. Considered to be both a process and an outcome, PTG is not the opposite of post-traumatic stress but can be experienced alongside it. To quote a common coaching maxim, breakdowns precede breakthroughs. The larger the breakdown, the more transformative the potential breakthrough.

Underscore 'potential'. In the realm of posttraumatic growth, the benefits of potential breakthroughs include a whole new experience of life — not just getting 'back to normal', but bouncing forward to an enhanced level of wellbeing surpassing any previous 'normal'.

This includes stronger self-esteem, more authentic relationships, a greater appreciation of 'the little things' and of life itself. It also includes expanded confidence for rising above future challenges … 'If I handled that, I can handle anything.' As my son Ben said after he graduated high school virtually in our living room during the COVID-19 pandemic, 'It takes a lot more to stress me out now.'

There's a distinct and important difference between responding to a situation and reacting to it. Responding well requires a clear head and calm hand to be thoughtful, reasoned and constructive. Reacting is driven by the fight-or-flight instinct, which drives us to lash out, shoot from the hip, retaliate or run for cover. In our conversations it compels us towards 'silence or violence', lurching reactively from one defensive position to another like an outmatched sword-bearer — all parry and no thrust.

Reacting is our default response. It's why those who cultivate emotional mastery are able to use their challenges as a lever to learn, grow and rise stronger. Little wonder EQ is a far stronger predictor of success than IQ. Working through the steps of the SOAR process will put you in a position to consciously choose how you will respond to any situation.

Of course, sometimes the choices you have available to deal with a situation aren't ones you feel are viable. For instance, a part of you may like nothing more than to tell your over-controlling, upwardly focused boss where to stick his job, but your family depends on your income and the impact of being out of work makes quitting your job, for now at least, not a viable option.

So when I refer to 'choice', I don't mean that all your choices are equal or even viable, but rather that you have the power to make them if you wish. Acknowledging that you do have options available to you, and consciously choosing which option you will take, will move you from a place of weakness and victimhood to one of power and ownership. As illustrated in figure 8, by actively choosing your response to a less-than-optimal situation — a stimulus — you'll shift the way you approach it and the spirit you bring to it.

Figure 8: the power of choice

For instance, if you're in a job you really don't enjoy, or working in a toxic team culture — but for various reasons you don't feel you can choose to leave right now — then you're still in a position to choose the attitude and spirit you'll bring to your role each day. Because you have the power to choose, you're only ever a victim of your environment if you choose to be. To quote the great philosopher Seneca, 'Most powerful is he who has himself in his own power.'

BREAKDOWNS PRECEDE BREAKTHROUGHS

Kintsugi is the ancient Japanese art of fixing cracked pottery. Rather than hide the cracks, the broken pieces are rejoined with lacquer mixed with powdered gold, silver or platinum. When restored, the pottery holds a new, unique beauty, one that embraces its past 'breakdown' for the beauty it holds. So embrace your breakdowns for the gifts they hold. And don't underestimate your capacity for adapting to change and turning your greatest challenges into a catalyst for your highest growth.

Taking yourself through each of the four SOAR steps isn't a one-off exercise in emotional mastery. It's a process you'll need to take yourself through again and again — sometimes for the very same problem or person! Just as a one-off walk along a new path through a forest doesn't create a new track, so too will you have to 'train your brain' to respond differently — with more calm, less angst. A note of warning: this will take longer than you'd like.

Truly successful people are those who have succeeded in mastering the game of life. They're fully engaged in living a life that matters, but they can also respond to their setbacks, struggles and sorrows from an enlarged perspective. They still feel the pain associated with everyday living, but they don't judge it as good or bad, rather as an invitation to feel more deeply and live more wholeheartedly. And while they may never have heard of the SOAR steps, they most certainly live them.

> **Choosing to walk the path of faith over fear, trusting that life isn't happening to you but *for* you, will help you find opportunity in every adversity.**

When storms blow in, oaks grow deeper roots. Likewise, adversity often compels us to look within for the certainty we cannot find elsewhere. In the process it introduces us to new dimensions of our own humanity and hones strengths that may otherwise have lain dormant. By challenging you to take another look at how you've been looking at your life it expands your bandwidth to thrive under pressure and lead yourself to higher ground.

This begs the question: if you trusted that whatever happened, you could handle it, how would that liberate you to soar to whole new heights?

7

LEAD BRAVELY

Cultivate a culture that fuels courage, not fear

To lead you must become comfortable being uncomfortable. You must be all-in, all the time. Inspire others to believe, then enable that belief to become reality.

GARY BURNISON, CEO, KORN FERRY

Once upon a time there was a leader who had risen through the ranks a rung too high — at least, too high for the good of anything but his ego. Let's call him Matt.

Deep within, Matt knew this to be true. Alas, his ego kept him from acknowledging what he did not know, much less asking for help. Insecure about his abilities, he overcompensated by puffing himself up. Yet he felt constantly on guard about his bluff being blown. As a result, he spent much of his time preoccupied with what could go wrong and working to protect his positional power.

He was anxious about anything he could not control, which was a lot. His identity and future were staked on the company division he ran, and he worried it would lose ground under his watch. He worked in fear, spoke with fear and led from fear. Over time, his fear seeped through into his management team, then filtered into the ranks beneath him, chipping away at the enthusiasm and courage of everyone in his organisation. No-one felt secure.

As Matt's anxiety grew, his judgement weakened. He cut spending. He micromanaged. He reworked his subordinates' presentations to management and filtered all upward feedback. He kept his cards to his chest and his plans even closer. He watched every move his team made and pushed out those who dared to challenge him — the best, the brightest and boldest. Those who remained learned it was best to nod and acquiesce. Over time, all initiative ceased. Distrust spread through the ranks as fear had before it.

Then crisis rocked his industry. Matt made major cuts. His tendency to 'play not to lose' magnified. All the while his company's more agile competitors innovated, gaining ground and then some. Under his watch, opportunities were squandered, commercial value was lost and potential held hostage by the fear he'd sown.

Once upon a time … aah … don't we wish.

While this story is largely fictitious (and Matt's resemblance to anyone in your workplace purely coincidental), this tale is not uncommon.

It's why this chapter is focused on helping you a) become a better leader who emboldens others to be braver, and b) not be a leader like Matt.

> People play safe when they feel unsafe to do otherwise. It is why creating a culture that fuels courage, not fear, is one of the most important tasks of leadership: a culture that emboldens people to be braver than their natural inclination. The first way leaders can do that is by being braver than *their own* inclination. Just as fear is contagious, so too is courage. People who are willing to lay their vulnerability on the line for the sake of a nobler cause will make it safer for others to do the same.

The biggest threat to any organisation is rarely the most visible. It's the fear that resides within its walls or over its Zoom-ways. As headlines blaze with news of restructures, AI-driven cutbacks and jobs offshored by labour arbitrage, fear can spread like a virus, driving clever, capable and creative people to make short-sighted decisions that work against the interests of their organisation. Why? Because people play safe unless they feel safe to do otherwise.

As our world has become increasingly interconnected, mobile, volatile and competitive, the need for leaders to embolden others to 'lean towards risk' and challenge old paradigms has become greater than ever. Those who step up to the challenge will stand out, and because they stand out they'll find themselves in a unique position to see opportunity where others see threats, to grow influence where others grow anxiety, and to plant seeds of courage in those around them where others plant only seeds of doubt.

Psychological safety has been found to be the strongest predictor of team success than any other factor, including collective IQ or diversity. This means how safe people feel to take interpersonal risks — such as challenging each other's opinions, sharing their own mistakes and misgivings, admitting that they don't know what to do, asking for help, or apologising when they have got something wrong.

> **People working in teams with high levels of psychological safety are not only more engaged, but collaborate better to foster synergies that unleash collective ingenuity. In short, they are stronger than the sum of the parts.**

In a psychologically safe environment, mistakes are not career-enders and failure becomes a valuable coach, teaching valuable lessons that only build edge. So when you make others feel respected and cared for, you encourage (en+*courage*) them to go forward and take risks. As Amy Edmondson wrote in *The Fearless Organization*, 'psychological safety takes off the brakes that keep people from achieving what's possible.'

In many ways, a leader acts as the emotional barometer for those around them, giving people cues on how to respond and react to situations. By tuning in and acknowledging the fears and anxieties of those around them, leaders can help people navigate their way through change and uncertainty more confidently. Even in the presence of fear, uncertainty and risk-averseness, they can help to cultivate a culture of courage.

Too often managers fixate on what will happen if people fail. How often have you heard others warn, 'If you screw up, you're a goner', or said to yourself, 'I'll die if I mess this up'? The problem is that the more attention we put on what may go wrong, the less we have left for what could go right. As Bill Treasurer wrote in *Courage Goes to Work*, 'By focusing solely on the consequences of failure, such managers are, in effect, widening the holes in the safety nets.'

This chapter is about helping you create the conditions for others to do their best work — to think bigger about the challenges you face and take the brave actions required to turn bold ideas into better outcomes.

So how can you do that?

Start where all meaningful change in the world outside you must stem from ... by taking a long hard look at the world within you!

REAL LEADERSHIP EXTENDS FROM THE INSIDE OUT

True leadership transcends the traditional 'command and control' ideas many of us were conditioned to associate with leadership — ideas of strong, competitive, domineering men standing on the mountaintop, directing all beneath them. In an era where companies are growing flatter, fewer leaders of the future will direct action from an ivory tower (and those who try to will fail). More and more will emerge from within the ranks. Both men and women, of every hue and background, whose actions are driven by a clear sense of purpose and intrinsic power — rather than by fear of losing power — will command the respect and grow the influence needed to shape the future: in business, government and society; locally, nationally and globally.

> **Leadership is not the domain of a few; it is the domain of anyone with the courage to act with it. So put aside your old paradigms of how leaders are supposed to look and take a look in the mirror. Yes, YOU have everything it takes to be a leader and the sooner you see yourself as one, the sooner others will too.**

The most successful leaders today are men and women who refuse to settle for mediocrity or cling to security. They speak candidly, embrace change and seize opportunity from adversity. They're willing to lay their career and bonus on the line for their vision and values. In doing so, they embody the courage mindset. Sometimes their actions produce extraordinary results; other times they fall short. But their ascent to the highest levels of power and influence isn't purely for the results they've produced. Rather, it's for their courage to challenge tradition, to hone their judgement through deep listening, embark on ambitious goals, execute them with tenacity and persevere amid adversity — all things that you can also do.

'Leaders are made, not born. And they are made more by themselves than by any external means. Everyone, at any age, is capable of self-transformation.' These words by renowned leadership expert Warren Bennis echo a timeless truth. While some people possess natural traits we tend to associate with leadership, the truth is that any person, at any age, at any level, in any-sized organisation can be a leader. And in today's increasingly uncertain and volatile environment, there has never been a greater need, nor more opportunity, for all people at all ages and at all levels in all organisations to step up to the plate of leadership, grow their sphere of influence, and own their power to make an impact.

While writing this book I was asked numerous times whether I was writing a leadership book or a personal-development book. Is there any meaningful difference?

Most of the 100 000-plus books on leadership are focused on the specific challenges and strategic choices of those in positions of formal 'leadership' authority. All well and good. But unless that person has first done the hard work of leading themselves, all the brilliant leadership advice in the world won't transform them into a great leader. It likely also explains why so many people who have been anointed as 'leaders' fall short when it comes to inspiring the best in those around them. They simply haven't done the hard 'inner' work to address the core fears and beliefs that mire the best in themselves. Leadership is all about personal development; it extends from the inside out.

A leader with unchallenged assumptions, unacknowledged insecurities, ungrounded stories, unbridled ego and unwillingness to listen will be limited in how they engage with those around them. This in turn will profoundly undermine their efforts to build trust, get buy-in and harness the full potential of those they lead.

You exert influence by virtue of the trust you build in your relationships. Where your currency of trust is weak, so too will be the results you can produce. Which begs the question, 'How can you build a solid network of trusting relationships that enables you to wield influence regardless of your authority?' While there are many different ways to answer that question, at the core of each lies your ability to create meaningful connections, to become a person that others can count on to say and do what's right — even when it costs you — and to be a person of true vision, character and courage others can look to for much-needed inspiration.

So, when you commit to playing a bigger game in your work, you also, by default, commit to being a leader. Leadership demands courage, and courage creates leaders.

> **Whatever your current level of authority, you can demonstrate leadership and positively influence those around you. You do it every time you act with the courage, purpose and passion you'd like to see more of in others. So ask yourself: 'If I was CEO, what would I want someone in my position to do?' By daring to step up and lead the change you know will serve the highest good, you inspire others to do the same.**

While there are countless models and theories on leadership, my experience working with organisations across cultures, countries and continents has taught me that the most useful paradigms are also the simplest. To that end, here's a simple model (as illustrated in figure 9) to help you lead more bravely. It consists of three intersecting domains – connect, inspire and embolden.

Connect — Establish authentic relationships with a high currency of trust.

Inspire — Engage people behind a meaningful and compelling vision with a big Why.

Embolden — cultivate a culture of courage that makes people feel safe to take risks.

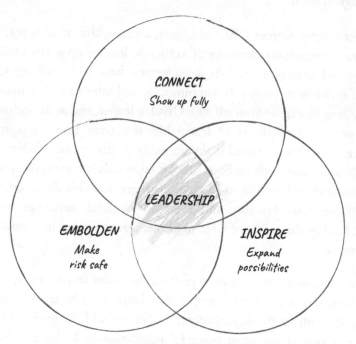

Figure 9: the three domains of courageous leadership

CONNECT AUTHENTICALLY

Before people decide what they think of a message, they decide what they think of the messenger. As such, establishing authentic relationships is crucial. The stronger your connections, the more influence you wield and the bigger impact you can make. Everything else hinges on that.

Daniel Goleman's research into emotional intelligence found that human beings are wired for connection: we not only *want* to belong and connect with others, we *need* to connect! We are at our best when we enjoy meaningful connections that go deeper than surface-level exchanges. But meaningful engagement can't occur unless we're connecting from a place of authenticity. Yet interacting and leading authentically is often an act of courage in itself.

As James Strong, former CEO of Qantas airlines, shared with me: 'One of the most important elements of authentic leadership is the ability to confront and overcome fear. As a leader you have to be willing to put yourself at risk in the way you communicate and interact with employees; to be willing to expose yourself as a CEO, a leader, and as an individual. Many people in positions of leadership shy away from engaging in unstructured and unprepared dialogue, easily justifying their failure to do so by the many demands on their time. It takes courage to expose yourself in an unstructured session of discussion where you risk direct criticism, difficult questions, hostility and even unsuccessful outcomes because you are leaving the safety of a scripted message delivered in a controlled environment.'

Finding the courage to step out of your comfort zone in your interpersonal interactions sets a powerful example that helps to cultivate a culture of courage throughout the organisation. As Strong said, 'Engaging in open dialogue is one of the most powerful interactions a leader can have. It makes a dramatic statement of respect and has an equally dramatic effect on leadership credibility. People notice when a leader puts themselves at risk and shows a genuine interest in people, their tasks, their contribution, their concerns and their problems. They also respect them more for doing so.'

The truth is that you lead by virtue of who you are, not where you got your MBA (or whether you got one at all!). Your power doesn't reside in being right, but in being real. In today's culture that is awash with the superficial, people are hungry for that which is real and authentic. We trust people who don't need to prove their superiority or protect their pride; people who show up as being fully 'human' rather than that little bit better than the rest of us.

The five ways you can engage authentically with those around you and unlock the collective potential of those around you are:

Listen authentically

Share authentically

Express authentically

Acknowledge authentically

Serve authentically

LISTEN AUTHENTICALLY: UNLOCK THE POWER OF PRESENCE

Most of us struggle to listen to people around us with the level of authenticity that makes them feel truly heard. That's because while we're pretending to listen, we're really just 'reloading', waiting for our turn to fire back our opinion to help them 'see the light'. But genuine listening is done not with the intention of being understood, but with the intention of understanding. Too few of us do it well.

When was the last time someone asked you how you were doing and then sat and listened to your response, without cutting in or interjecting their own thoughts, opinions or suggestions? Putting aside the time to listen to someone is an act of generosity. It validates who they are in ways that nothing else can. It also helps you appreciate the world they're living in, which, while it may have a lot of outward similarities to your own, may be starkly different from yours.

Listening is often underrated, yet it's the most powerful tool in any leader's toolkit. Listening authentically impacts the quality of every career and business relationship you have. It breaks down the barriers that keep people from being able to trust and collaborate in the best way. It provides a means to grow powerful, collaborative relationships and optimise cooperation with your co-workers, clients, suppliers and employees.

When you lecture, explain or prescribe without first listening, you alienate people and raise their defences. But when you try to understand their perspective and listen in a respectful, sincere way, you can enrol others in your goals and vision and influence change in ways that those who fail to listen never can.

Who in your orbit would value you taking time today to listen to them?

SHARE AUTHENTICALLY: UNLOCK THE POWER OF VULNERABILITY

Lowering your 'let-me-look-leader-like' mask and allowing yourself to be truly vulnerable with colleagues and employees lays at the foundation of true connection, open communication and collaboration. As Howard Shultz, CEO of Starbucks, once said, 'The hardest thing about being a leader is demonstrating or showing vulnerability.' Yet as Shultz wrote in *From The Ground Up*, vulnerability 'brings people and teams together'.

Sharing yourself authentically — revealing your humanity — is like investing in the stock market: you can't benefit from the upside (open, caring and trust-filled relationships) without also having the downside (vulnerability). Leaders to whom others can relate as fellow human beings — rather than simply as people with the power to cut their budget or outsource their job — are able to engage employees and raise performance. As Harvard researcher Shawn Achor wrote in his book *The Happiness Advantage*, 'The more genuinely expressive someone is, the more their mindset and feelings spread.'

Mother Teresa, respected the world over for her raw courage and lack of pretension, once said, 'Honesty and transparency make you vulnerable. Be honest and transparent anyway.' The word 'vulnerable' carries a negative connotation, but it's through becoming vulnerable that we can connect most deeply with others. That said, I want to be clear that vulnerability does not equate to weakness or limitation. No leader in their right mind would advocate a weak position on the market battlefield or want those around them to look weak. Quite the opposite: strength of character and position are critical in balancing vulnerability.

Sharing yourself authentically can run against your protective instincts. This explains why, when you anticipate finding yourself in a vulnerable predicament, your automatic reaction is to put up your guard and protect yourself: to pull out of the launch, cancel the meeting, step back from the relationship or retreat from centre stage.

> Allowing yourself to be vulnerable is counterintuitive. It's also how you connect most deeply to other people. We connect far more deeply through our struggles and vulnerability than our successes and victories. Genuine leadership calls for us to embrace our vulnerability, not only so that we can connect more authentically with the people around us, but so that we can inspire them to embrace their own vulnerability.

By revealing your humanity you can create trusting relationships in your team in a way that showing only your strengths never can. As Patrick Lencioni wrote in *The Five Dysfunctions of a Team*, 'vulnerability is not a soft skill. It's the key to building great teams.'

Where are you wearing a mask to protect your vulnerability? How might lowering it enable you to connect more meaningfully with those around you? What relationships might blossom if you lowered it?

EXPRESS AUTHENTICALLY: UNLOCK THE POWER OF DIVERSITY

Your brand is the unique promise you make to your organisation, clients and colleagues. You build your brand in every interaction, conversation and action — from the most mundane to the most significant.

Priscilla Bryans, a partner at Herbert Smith Freehills law firm, shared with me her journey of learning to simply be herself. An extrovert by nature, she felt early in her career that she needed to be more like the many introverts she worked with in order to succeed. For years she was concerned that others wouldn't take her seriously and that acting like herself could impede her career. But over time Priscilla discovered that by daring to express herself authentically, as vulnerable as that initially made her feel, she was able to forge more meaningful relationships.

When all you do is conform, all you have to offer is conformity; when all you do is try to fit in, you negate the difference your difference makes. All the while you deprive your co-workers, your clients and company of the full quota of unique value that you have to contribute. Ironically, when you're preoccupied with a need to impress people, the impression you usually make is a far cry from the one you want.

If I were to go into your workplace and ask everyone you interact with what words come to mind when they think of you, what common attributes do you think would come up again and again? If I were to do the same for everyone else in your organisation, what would stand out about you that would differentiate you from others?

Authentic self-expression is about embracing what makes you unique and refusing to succumb to the lure of conformity. Owning what makes you different enables you to differentiate yourself and build a strong personal brand. While it's important to be attuned to how others are perceiving you, when you allow their opinions (or what you think they think) to determine how you show up — what you say or do — you dilute the value you bring.

Coco Chanel said, 'In order to be irreplaceable, one must always be different.' Expressing yourself authentically is about owning what makes you different and refusing to conform to an expectation of how you 'should' be. Authentic self-expression is what enables you to build your own brand of brilliance.

Every interaction and conversation you have — from the most mundane (passing someone in the hallway on your way to the copy machine) to the most significant (presenting to the board) — shapes and builds Brand You Inc.

Social psychologists have found that two out of three people are out of touch with how others see them compared to how they see themselves, the irony being that people who strive the hardest to be liked or to impress others often have the opposite effect on those around them. People can intuitively sense insincerity or a lack of congruence in someone even when they can't put their finger on what's missing. Expressing yourself authentically requires not letting others' opinions matter more than your own, particularly given that your assumptions about what other people are thinking are so often off the mark. As Dr Seuss so wisely said, 'Be who you are and say what you feel because those who mind don't matter and those who matter don't mind.'

ACKNOWLEDGE AUTHENTICALLY: UNLOCK THE POWER OF APPRECIATION

It's easy to criticise others. Many people are exceptionally talented at it. But while constructive criticism — delivered in the right way at the right time — has its place, to be effective it must be balanced with hearty doses of praise, appreciation and acknowledgement.

A few years ago I spoke at an event with Jim Clifton, CEO and chairman of Gallup. Sharing the lessons he had learned over his career, he encouraged the audience to focus on their strengths — on what they're naturally good at — and less on their weaknesses. Drawing on research by Gallup, he explained how people succeed more from leveraging their natural strengths than by trying to shore up their weaknesses (beyond the point of them not tripping them up). Given that a recent Gallup survey found that only 11 per cent of employees worldwide are engaged in their jobs, it seems that one of the most tangible ways leaders can boost engagement is to help employees discover their strengths. This begins by acknowledging them.

Leaders — from team supervisors to C-Suite executives — are constantly on the alert for behaviours that might jeopardise team results. But keeping people focused on strengthening their weaknesses can come at the cost of not gaining the full benefit of their strengths. As attention and effort is invested in bolstering weakness, natural strengths atrophy. Finding the right balance is an ongoing challenge, but there is no better place to start than by acknowledging and celebrating what they do well.

In *Why Marriages Succeed or Fail,* John Gottman found that relationships that had a 5:1 ratio of appreciation to criticism were the most healthy, happy and productive. Relationships that were at or below a 1:1 ratio of appreciation to criticism were headed towards failure. His ability to predict divorce based on his observations of how couples communicated was alarmingly accurate (better than 90 per cent!). Work relationships are not dissimilar.

Many people go to work each day not feeling that their strengths, efforts and accomplishments are valued fully by those around them. Too few are encouraged to focus on them. Acknowledging authentically means taking time out from your busyness to focus on what people are doing well and acknowledging them for it. Don't be limited to a result that someone has achieved. Focus on the virtues they've brought to the task at hand: perseverance, collaboration, a sense of humour, tenacity, resilience, initiative, creativity, assertiveness, flexibility, strong organisation or a great work ethic. Often we assume that others don't need our affirmation in order to know they've done a good job, yet I have yet to see a pat on the back go unappreciated. To quote entrepreneur and Net-a-Porter co-founder, Megan Quinn: 'Everyone likes to feel part of a tribe, nurtured and celebrated.'

> Actively supporting people in good times places big deposits into the relational bank account, which you can draw from in difficult times. If people feel you've been good to them when you haven't needed to, they'll go the extra mile when you need them.

SERVE AUTHENTICALLY: UNLOCK THE POWER OF LOVE

Martin Luther King Jr once said that 'life's most persistent and urgent question is: What are you doing for others?'

If you asked yourself this question every day, and acted on the answer, you would be an incredible leader. Unfortunately, it's not near common enough. Again, our fear-driven egos have a lot to answer for here. A Gallup study found that employees who feel cared for are more productive, more profitable and less likely to jump ship when another offer comes along. So when you engage with others from a place of service, making them feel cared for is not only a nice thing to do; it's smart for business.

In *Leadership from the Inside Out* Kevin Cashman wrote, 'Ultimately a leader is not judged so much by how well he or she leads, but by how well he or she serves. All value and contribution are achieved through service.' In other words, it's not about being self-centred, but being other-centred. Of course, while it's a noble goal to approach leadership from a place of loving service, in our desire to achieve more success we're often drawn away from serving others to serving ourselves. We are, after all, human beings. The more you remember that it's about them, not you, the more effective you'll be as a leader.

Regardless of its size, no carrot or stick will ever trump the effect you have on those around you when you engage with them from a place of service. So take a moment to reflect on these questions:

What experience do people have of working and interacting with me?

How do others feel when they're in my presence?

How would I engage differently if I focused on what I can give versus what I can get?

INSPIRE POSSIBILITIES

My friend Jim Kouzes wrote in *The Leadership Challenge* (co-authored with Barry Posner) that: 'There's nothing more demoralizing than a leader who can't clearly articulate why we're doing what we're doing. It's true. Leaders need to not only inspire people with a vision. A leader who can't do that is a little like a river without water, dry and depressing.'

Leaders paint a picture of the future before it arrives. One that inspires people at a deep human level, nurturing the diversity in their ranks and tapping into their desire to make their own unique mark in their own unique way.

In today's climate of fear, the need for inspiration is greater than ever. You inspire greatness by reminding people of what's at stake, connecting them to the purpose underlying what they're doing and elevating your expectations of them.

> **Traditional carrot-and-stick approaches to leadership can produce results. But they're limited by the size of the carrot and the length of the stick. As such, they're not sustainable. The most powerful motivating force, once our basic needs are met, is fulfilling the innate desire for meaning: truly believing that our hard work is 'work worth doing'.**

While spirituality and business may seem an oxymoron, organisations that can connect their employees to a bigger purpose — to a *why* that transcends their pay cheque — are those that can retain and inspire employees to continually go the extra mile, not for the prize of recognition or promotion, but for the fulfilment they get from achieving something worthwhile and personally meaningful.

Leaders help remind people what's at stake, not just in terms of bottom-line profitability, but in terms of growing into their fullest potential.

Martin Luther King Jr's 'I Have a Dream' speech connected millions of people with a bigger vision, a bigger purpose, a bigger why. While King's speech rallied people behind a cause, if you listen to the background audio you can hear the muffled sounds of the many hundreds of thousands at the Lincoln Memorial on that humid August day clapping, hollering and shouting, 'Amen', 'Oh, yes', and 'Alleluia brother'.

King connected them to a vision they had not dared to dream for themselves. He tapped into their sadness, their anger and their fear. Most of all he tapped into their hope that the future could be brighter than the past. The Black Lives Matter protests that sprang up around America and inspired rallies across the globe in 2020 tell us that King's dream has yet to be realised. Yet they also tell us that when people are inspired by the future vision of what is possible, it unlocks possibilities that may otherwise have lain dormant.

> Great leaders don't just manage 'what is' but work towards 'what could be', painting a picture for the future before it arrives. They don't permit what's probable to limit pursuing what's possible. Rather, by focusing on an 'invented future' that is unconstrained by what has come before, leaders rally people to pull together, dig deeper and move forward more boldly, bound by common purpose.

The great French writer and aviator Antoine de Saint-Exupery once said, 'If you want to build a ship, don't drum up people to collect wood and don't assign them tasks and work but rather teach them to long for the endless immensity of the sea.' His words tap into a deep longing we all have for greatness. You inspire greatness when you help people move up from 'what is now' — often a place lacking in ambition, where decisions are driven by fear rather than inspiration or ambition — to 'what could be': a place of possibility, purpose and courage. Figure 10 (overleaf) illustrates this.

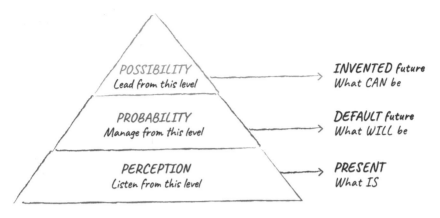

Figure 10: leaders can see what can be

Level 1: Seeing what is now through the eyes of reality. This is the level of perception. A leader listens from this level.

Level 2: Seeing what will be through the eyes of discernment. This is the level of probability. A leader manages from this level.

Level 3: Seeing what can be through the eyes of vision. This is the level of possibility. A leader lives and inspires from this level.

In ancient Greek mythology, Pygmalion was a Cypriot sculptor who carved an ivory sculpture of his ideal woman. Pygmalion fell in love with the statue, naming her Galatea, and made an offering at the altar of Venus, wishing that his sculpture would become a real woman. Venus granted Pygmalion his heart's desire, and so, according to the Roman poet Ovid, Pygmalion went on to marry Galatea and they lived happily ever after.

Psychologists have borrowed from Greek mythology to describe the impact of positive expectation, which they've called the Pygmalion effect. It is a simple and effective way to boost performance in the classroom, the workplace, the military and elsewhere. In the realm of leadership, when you believe in the potential of those around you to make a meaningful contribution and ascend to greatness in their own right, you set the stage for them to do just that. The Pygmalion effect was first studied in the famous experiment by psychologist Robert Rosenthal on primary-school students.

Rosenthal led teachers to believe that certain students in their classrooms had been identified as 'intellectual bloomers', children who would show an intellectual growth spurt during the school year. In fact, the students were randomly given the designation of intellectual bloomers, but at the end of the term they did indeed show higher academic achievement. Why? Because the teachers believed in them. How? Later studies showed that teachers unconsciously gave more positive attention, feedback and learning opportunities to these students. In short, teachers were able to nonverbally communicate their positive expectations for academic success to these students.

Professor Dov Eden from Tel Aviv University went on to demonstrate the Pygmalion effect in all sorts of work groups, across all sectors and industries. If supervisors or managers hold positive expectations about the performance of those they lead — for example, by believing they can solve a challenging problem — performance improves. A meta-analysis found Pygmalion leadership training to be a highly effective leadership-development intervention.

On the other hand, if the leader holds negative expectations — anticipating that their team or group will fail — performance weakens. This has been called the Golem effect. It's where lowering the expectations of people (including ourselves!) leads to poorer performance. Both the Pygmalion and Golem effects are forms of self-fulfilling prophecy. To summarise: Expect much, get more. Expect little, get less.

Of course, expecting that everyone in every situation will meet or exceed your expectations is naive. Just as you don't always act with the level of courage, commitment and character that you aspire to, so too will others sometimes falter and fall short. Don't be blind to obvious inconsistencies in behaviour. Blind trust is foolish. Rather, trust that people, by and large, are good, mean well and have within them the resources to solve their own problems. Likewise, trust your intuition when something feels amiss.

Whether you're a leader of two or 2000, when you expect more from those you work with, you can do more yourself.

As you move up into roles with greater demands and responsibilities, you'll become more discerning about how you spend your time. The challenge for many people who rise up from the ranks of a solo contributor into a managerial role is to 'get out of the weeds' and delegate more to others. While delegating may not seem like a particularly brave thing to do, it can be for people who fear that the potentially substandard work of others will impact their reputation and success. There's no getting away from it: delegating and outsourcing involves risk. However, in failing to delegate you can run the greater risk of failing to deliver what's expected of you.

David Ogilvy, founder of the giant advertising agency Ogilvy, used to give each new manager a Russian doll containing five progressively smaller dolls. He put a message inside the smallest one that read, 'If each of us hires people we consider smaller than ourselves, we shall become a company of dwarves. But if each of us hires people who are bigger than we are, we will become a company of giants.' Beyond the need to hire people who have skills and talents that complement and exceed our own is the need to inspire those we already work with to use their skills and talents in ways that complement and exceed our own, by inspiring them to greatness.

The focus of a leader should be to build big people, because big people take bolder actions and handle problems in better ways. When you trust others to get on with their job, it elevates their performance. When you micromanage and fail to trust them to perform within their ability, it undermines it. While giving people extra responsibility and involvement in decision-making increases the risk, it also increases their engagement. Delegation is therefore one of the most powerful managerial tools for increasing productivity and emboldening others to 'train the brave' and build their courage muscles in their work and life.

EMBOLDEN PEOPLE TO TAKE BRAVER ACTION

The number-one role of leaders is to make risk safe — to create the conditions for others to bring their boldest thinking to the challenges at hand and to embolden them to take the brave actions needed to turn ideas into outcomes. So in today's fearful environment, fostering a culture of courage where people feel safe and inspired to take risks, to innovate and to experiment, is mission critical.

To do that effectively leaders have to consider the two ecosystems that impact how the people around them think, feel and act:

internal ecosystem — what's going on inside us

external ecosystem — what's going on around us.

> To create a culture of courage in your team or organisation you need to ensure people feel safe to push the envelope of what's possible — to challenge old thinking, experiment with new ideas and to step onto fresh ground. Unless people feel they're able to make the odd bad decision, they will never be free to make good ones. Smart risks lead to smart mistakes, and smart mistakes are an invaluable part of the learning process.

People feel safe when they know that if what they try doesn't work out, they won't have to walk out the door. Reassuring people that their risks won't be punished — assuming they're doing their homework and not being reckless or foolhardy — helps to offset their fear and promote their willingness to try new things.

In *Emotional Intelligence*, Daniel Goleman wrote, 'Like second-hand smoke, the leakage of emotions can make a bystander an innocent casualty of someone else's toxic state.' As a leader, you have the responsibility to ensure that whatever emotions you're spreading, they're setting others up to be more successful, not less; more confident, not less; more calm, not less; more adaptable, not less; and more willing to do whatever it takes to find opportunity in adversity and to go the extra mile when the extra mile counts.

An employee survey of 1000 US employees from a diverse range of companies in early 2021 found that employees who had already been working in the physical workplace during the pandemic were far more comfortable with returning to work full time in their workplaces than those who had been working remotely during the pandemic. Those who had been going to work were far more comfortable in the measures their companies had taken to provide safe workplaces for when everyone returned. Those who had been at home were far more anxious about their safety upon returning. The contrast can be explained by a term called the 'mere exposure effect':

> **The 'mere exposure effect' explains why the more often someone is 'merely exposed' to a situation that can engender fear, the less fearful they feel and the more normalised it becomes. In the same way, the more often people are exposed to situations outside their psychological comfort zone, the more comfortable they become with them.**

Bomb-disposal experts, when given both the right training to disarm highly explosive bombs and sufficient practice at doing it, are able to handle situations that would frighten the socks off most people — with extraordinary calm. Helping people build competence through developing new skills and increasing their exposure to new situations reduces their fear of failure. In doing so, you create scaffolding that builds their confidence to take bolder actions in the future.

When asked what courageous leadership looks like, Kate Johnson, president of the $45-billion division of Microsoft US, replied, 'When you see a person trying to get it right, instead of trying to be right.' By role-modelling working to 'get it right' versus trying to 'be right', you make it safer for others to exit their comfort zone and try new things. Ongoing experimentation increases the odds of finding and developing better ways of doing things that help to build competitive edge. Of course, experimentation can't take place without mistakes, so organisations must be willing to make them.

One client shared with me that when he sees people who never make mistakes, it's a sign that they have become too comfortable: 'If people are going to be ready for bigger jobs, they have to be put into roles that have some element of risk. Even if managed carefully, there is always some risk.'

He added, 'We all have to be willing to stretch ourselves, or we will never know how much we can do, and neither will anyone else. Of course it's also important to have safeguards so any mistakes do not put at risk the safety, security and financial viability of the operation.'

> **Courage is one of the most important values to be embedded in an organisation's cultural DNA. While courage doesn't guarantee success, it always precedes it. So reward it accordingly. After all, if leaders are preoccupied with avoiding failure, they enlarge the holes in people's psychological safety net. This stifles the very creativity, innovation and experimentation needed to forge new ground and build stronger edge.**

In *How Winning Leaders Make Great Calls*, Noel Tichy and Warren Bennis wrote, 'Courageous leaders often get their courage from their fear about what will happen if they don't step up and boldly step out.'

Sometimes people are afraid, but they're not sure what they're afraid of. Sure, they're scared that something will change or that they might fail or that they might lose their job. But what fears lie beneath the obvious? What is it about change that makes them so fearful? What is it about losing their job or being passed over for promotion that gives rise to their anxiety? As I shared in chapter 2, fear of the consequences of failing to act can be a great motivator in getting the job done quickly and efficiently.

In his book *Peak Performers*, Charles Garfield says that peak performers are able to ask themselves the questions, 'What's the worst that could happen?' and 'What would I do if the worst actually did happen?'. Helping those around you explore those two questions lowers the perceived risk and helps to harness the energy of fear to move forward.

Likewise, it's important to acknowledge people when they act courageously, even when their actions don't produce the outcome they want. When you reward courageous behaviours — not just successful ones — you're also demonstrating to everyone the values you want them to adopt, and teaching them the value you place on those who refuse to stick with status-quo thinking and play safe. After all, while courage doesn't guarantee success, it always precedes it.

The reward doesn't have to be a trophy or a bonus; it could be a hand-written note from a manager, a pat on the back or a story shared at a team meeting in front of peers. The type of reward doesn't matter so long as it's meaningful to the person receiving it and is linked to the emboldened behaviour you want to encourage.

AMPLIFY THE RIPPLE EFFECT

Fear is contagious. So too is courage. By daring to lean towards risk and choose courage over comfort, you embolden others to do the same. So ask yourself, 'What does the brave leader within me want me to do right now?' Act on the answer. Everything else will flow from there. Your example will always speak more loudly than your words.

Of course, it's impossible to know, much less to measure, the impact that you can make on the lives of those around you by how you choose to show up each day. But every interaction you have with another human being involves an exchange of energy, influencing their emotional state in some way. Likewise every workplace develops what psychologists call a 'group affective tone'. Over time, 'emotional norms' are established and prolif-erate, reinforced by the behaviours — verbal and nonverbal — of those within the group (team or organisation). So the good news is that what-ever your position, you can affect the emotional tone of those around you.

Any time you drop an object into water, you witness the ripple effect. However small the object, by piercing the surface of the water it sets off an energy force within the body of water that extends outwards. When you choose to step up to the leadership plate, you do the same.

PART III

TAKE COURAGE

SET YOURSELF UP FOR SUCCESS!

Playing safe is probably the most unsafe thing in the world. You cannot stand still. You must go forward.

ROBERT COLLIER

8

BACK YOURSELF

Don't wait to feel brave ... take the leap!

Until one is committed there is hesitancy, a chance to draw back. Boldness has genius, power and magic in it. Begin it now.

GOETHE

In ancient Rome, a centurion had the power to command those who were not Roman citizens to carry his equipment for a mile. At first the conquered people of Rome's expansive empire resented being forced to carry the load of a Roman centurion and would go only as far as needed to avoid a brutal beating or even death. But in the first century Christians began the tradition of 'going the extra mile'. Not only would they do what was a forced necessity, but they would do more ... by choice.

Two thousand years later, the saying 'go the extra mile' has become a powerful philosophy. The idea of not just exerting the minimal effort required to 'get by', but of intentionally 'going the extra mile', has become a hallmark behaviour of successful people the world over. While the marketplace of mediocrity is a crowded space, it's never crowded on the extra mile. That's because going the extra mile takes extra commitment, hard work and sacrifice above that needed to 'get by'. Which is what this chapter is about: helping you identify the 'extra' actions you can take to set yourself up.

DARE TO MAKE THE ULTIMATE BET ... ON YOURSELF

Albert Einstein said, 'Nothing happens until something moves.' Unlocking the power of courage to create positive movement and momentum in your life takes more than a one-off decision to rethink risk and take bolder actions. It necessitates a commitment to 'going the extra mile' in how you live your life — not succumbing to the excuses, justifications and pressures that can so easily pull you out of action and back into playing safe and living smaller than serves you or anyone else.

While reading this book you have likely had numerous insights on things you could do differently. Insights are nice. They can even be useful. But unless acted upon, they're useless. Taking a bold leap of faith through your fears and beyond the familiar is where the rubber hits the road. It's where you put your commitment to the test as you move from thinking about what you *could* do, to actually doing it. This is where you reclaim the power that fear and self-doubt have had in your work, relationships and life as you build your own brand of courage.

Rowena Clift is executive director of a large regional hospital in Ballarat, Australia. Rowena began her career as a general nurse and moved into administration, working her way up to the role she's in today, where she ensures that patient care is coordinated across the various hospital departments. Rowena shared with me that she has always felt called to a vocation to care for people in need of medical help, and does her job with a strong sense of purpose. She also shared the motto that has guided her decisions throughout her career: 'no monkey grip'.

Early in her career Rowena realised that to make the maximum impact she wanted to make, she had to be ready to let go of doing purely clinical patient care. She told me, 'You have to be willing to trust, invest and be true to your vision. Otherwise fear of not having what it takes to "make it" on a new branch can hold you back.'

Just as monkeys can't make their way across a rainforest canopy without continuously letting go of the branch they're holding onto, neither can you reach out towards a future that inspires you with both hands holding tightly onto the security of where you are now ... in a tight monkey grip. You have to make an important decision: to trade the safety and familiarity of your present situation for the possibility of something better, despite the uncertainty that invites into your life.

> As we journey through life we will all arrive at crossroads that call on us to decide whether to trade the comfortable familiarity of where we are now for the possibilities we want most. The desire for comfort will always pull hard against the desire for growth.

In the end, that's what courage is all about: consciously deciding to make yourself vulnerable to all you fear so that you can bloom into the fullest expression of who you are, more powerful than any fear you'll ever have. Will that be scary sometimes? You bet. And when it is, just feel your fear, acknowledge it, then loosen its grip on the security of where you are now. Only then can you step towards the future you want and discover just what mettle you are made of.

To help you do that, it's vital to create an environment around you to support you in being the person you aspire to be. Never underestimate the power of your environment to help or hinder you in achieving the success you want, and being the person you need to be to achieve it.

ENLIST THE SUPPORT OF PEOPLE WHO LIFT YOU UP AND ENLARGE YOUR THINKING

While no-one is responsible for your success but you, you'll go much further and faster with the support of other people than alone. Designing an environment that sets you up to succeed means actively building a strong network of caring, confident and encouraging people you can reach out to for support, advice, or to give you a kick in the pants when you need it. When you're surrounded by people who believe in you and the value you have to contribute, it creates an environment that makes success easier to achieve. As Ita Buttrose, an icon in Australian media, shared with me: 'No person is an island. We all need help to get ahead.'

So many of the most successful people I've met over the years have shared similar sentiments. My friend Joan Amble is a former executive vice president of American Express and co-founder and chair of WOMEN in America, an organisation focused on supporting more women into the senior executive ranks of Fortune 500 corporations. She often tells women to build their own personal board of directors, made up of diverse people with relevant experience, insight and wisdom who are willing to tell them what they should hear — not just what they want to hear.

Creating your own board of directors can make a huge difference as you advance in your career. They can help you stay focused on what matters most, make optimal decisions when you come to a crossroads, better navigate new and uncertain territory in your career and remind you of your value if ever you come to doubt it.

Whatever you do, don't go it alone. To quote an African proverb: 'If you want to go fast, go alone. If you want to go far, go together.' Other people can support and help you do things that you can't do yourself. So engage a coach, find a mentor, join a professional association, enlist a trusted friend to hold you accountable, or create your own board of directors or mastermind group. Not only can these people expand your perspective and focus your resources on the highest-leverage activities, but many (particularly those within your industry) can also make valuable introductions that can open doors to new relationships and opportunities.

PRUNE YOUR TREE AND NEVER SHRINK YOURSELF DOWN TO MAKE OTHERS FEEL BETTER

Nick, a colleague who runs a consulting business, keeps a picture on his desk of a huge tree with three words underneath it: PRUNE YOUR TREE. The picture helps to remind him to always make sure to prune the clients and business relationships that are no longer ripe with opportunity. He's learned from some less-than-enjoyable experiences of staying in relationships that distracted his focus, weighed him down and on a few occasions set his business back financially. Likewise, when you 'prune your tree' of those people who drag you down or limit your ability to provide the value you want in your career, it doesn't make your life smaller. Rather, it creates space for more rewarding relationships to grow and more fruitful opportunities to emerge.

If you can't prune emotional vampires out of your life (sometimes you're related to them!) or exit a toxic environment where they abound, at least become more vigilant and limit contact as much as possible. Like inhaling second-hand smoke, it's easy to become a casualty to the toxic mindsets of other people if you're not paying attention.

Likewise, be wary of those people in your work or social environment who may feel threatened by your desire for change. As you go about changing how you engage in your work and in the world, you may find an almost magnetic force pulling you back into your habitual default ways of thinking and acting. Prepare yourself. People have grown accustomed to relating to you in a specific way. They expect you to act in certain ways and conform to the expectations they have of you. When you begin to step out and speak out, sometimes friction will ensue. Remember it's generally about them, not you. So never give other people's beliefs and insecurities about what they're doing with their own life the power to undermine what you're doing with yours.

Sometimes you need to let go of old relationships in order to grow. Don't let others play you small or pressure you to suppress who you are and who you want to become. As my friend Marianne Williamson wrote in *A Return to Love*, 'Your playing small does not serve the world. There is nothing enlightened about shrinking so that other people won't feel insecure around you.'

CLEAR YOUR CLUTTER: A PLACE FOR EVERYTHING AND EVERYTHING IN ITS PLACE

While it's important to be mindful of your social and emotional environment, your physical environment can also undermine your ability to be courageous in what you do and productive in how you do it. Disorganised people who work and live in chaos simply can't be as focused, purposeful and productive as organised people are.

The Pentagon Federal Credit Union (PenFed) engaged me to run a leadership-development program for its employees at its biggest offices across America. Before designing the program, I met up with the CEO, James Schenk, to discuss what they wanted to achieve and how I could optimise the impact on their business.

On arriving in James's office I noticed how many piles of paper he had around his desk. I couldn't help but smile as we shook hands and he gestured for me to take a seat at a table. Noticing the expression on my face he looked over to his cluttered desk and then back at me.

'It's organised chaos,' he assured me with a grin that told me he knew I wouldn't be convinced. 'That's what everyone with a messy desk says, James,' I joked. I then told him about a study that found that when people with offices that resembled his own were forced to put everything into a filing system, their productivity went up by between 40 and 60 per cent. He raised his eyebrows and promised me he'd clean it up before my next visit.

About three months later I returned to PenFed's head office to run a workshop. On seeing me, James proudly told me that his office was the picture of organisation. He went on to admit that his productivity had improved so much he even tidied up his closet at home!

> Clutter in *any* area of your life creates clutter in *every* area of your life. Piles of 'stuff' (clothes, documents, emails) don't help you succeed; they keep you stuck in head-spinning, tail-chasing, chaos. So before you set off on your next adventure, get your base camp in order.

CREATE RITUALS THAT EXPAND YOUR CAPACITY TO THRIVE UNDER PRESSURE

Resilience isn't what you have, it's what you do.

Successful people do things others don't. One of them is incorporating regular rituals and habits into their lives that enable them to maintain physical energy, mental focus and the emotional wellbeing to stay on track towards their goals, 'go the extra mile' as often as needed and take new challenges in their stride. They know that who they are is what they repeatedly do and that small, daily actions, repeated often, can make a profound difference.

Cultivating rituals that bolster resilience and build stamina will expand your capacity for accurately assessing risk, taking action and 'bounding forward' after setbacks.

Research has found that taking time out to disengage from your work to engage in other activities — whether to rest, exercise or pursue a hobby or creative pursuit — actually improves our effectiveness and productivity during the time we are engaged in our work.

As exhilarating and rewarding as it can be to face your fears, stepping out of your comfort zone can also tax your energy. Daring to change the status quo can be as demanding physically as it is mentally and emotionally. Leading a team of people through change and uncertainty is no less demanding. Indeed, the more you want to take on in your work, the more important it is for you to invest in regular rituals that 'top you up' and ensure you're operating with optimal levels of health and wellbeing in body, mind and spirit.

Psychologists estimate that 95 per cent of what we do on any given day is habitual and that only 5 per cent is done consciously. Expand your capacity to stay focused, fearless and thriving under pressure by developing habits that help you keep stress in check. So if you're feeling overwhelmed, anxious or just not on your game, it's not because of the load you are carrying but how you are carrying it. Prioritising empowering practices and habits will expand your bandwidth to thrive under pressure. The busier you are, the more crucial this becomes. Remember, you make your habits then your habits make you.

While your rituals are personal to you, people everywhere benefit from incorporating certain habits into their life — whether it be reading something uplifting during quiet time at the start or end of each day, writing down your day's priorities, working off the stress of a pressure-laden job in a morning run, journalling, reconnecting with your kids at a Friday night movie, making regular time for prayer or meditation, cycling with friends at the weekend, or walking through a nearby park at lunchtime. All these things can help you sustain the perspective, energy, focus and motivation to keep acting consistently and achieve the success you want. As Jim Loehr and Tony Schwartz wrote in *The Power of Full Engagement*, managing energy, not time, is crucial to success in today's high-pressure and competitive workplace.

Take a minute right now to think about what you could do more often that would help you do everything better, including taking the brave actions needed to keep moving onto higher ground in your work, leadership and life.

Think about something you could do weekly that you're currently not doing, but that you know will help you maintain the focus, energy and inspiration you need to stay engaged and in action over the longer haul.

Physically. Physical strength promotes psychological strength. What will you do on a regular basis to stay physically strong, energised and healthy?

Mentally. What will you do to focus your time and energy on what makes the biggest impact and brings the most value?

Emotionally. Emotions drive action, not logic. What can you do to process the negative emotions that keep you from engaging in the world with greater optimism, clarity and courage?

Spiritually. What small rituals help you live on purpose and stay more connected to your deeper 'reason for being', your highest why?

BUILD COURAGE IN INCREMENTS

Maria Eitel, founder and chair of Nike Foundation, told me how she learned to become comfortable with the discomfort of fear. When she was young her dad and older brother Nick would take her hiking. Describing herself as a 'skinny beanpole and not particularly strong', she said the hikes took her way outside her comfort zone as they were often long and demanding. At the end of one of their regular hiking paths they would arrive at a cliff overlooking a lake. Maria would be filled with fear as she stood on the cliff top looking down at the water, but her brother wouldn't let her off the hook by allowing her to take the easier, less intimidating path of clambering down the side of the cliff and entering the lake along the shoreline. So, despite feeling filled with fear, on the urging of her brother and dad she'd take a giant jump into the air and splash into the water below.

Certainly Maria's early childhood experiences taught her how to manage the physical sensation of fear and take bold and focused action in its presence.

'Courage is not one moment; it's a sequence of moments where you have to keep drawing from a reservoir of courage that's surrounded by a pool of fear. You have to keep tapping and tapping it day by day, moment by moment, and not let your fear overtake you,' she said to me. 'Coming from a position of fear, of not succeeding, losing your job or not being admired, handicaps the potential of your career. I've never let my fear of losing my job keep me from doing something I knew was the right thing to do.'

Today Maria continues to push through the very human fears and doubts that handicap many people in their careers. She leads the Nike Foundation's efforts to get girls onto the global agenda and drive resources to them with the goal of eradicating global poverty, something which requires her to make a stand for the greatness of women around the world every day.

Action is the most potent antidote to fear: it breeds confidence and nurtures courage in ways nothing else can. The more you step out of your comfort zone into your courage zone, the more you build your tolerance for risk and the confidence to handle its consequences. Don't wait to feel brave to act bravely. Courage begets courage. So dare to 'train the brave' in small ways and large. The more you act with the courage you wish you had, the braver you'll become.

One of the biggest obstacles you have to overcome as you connect to the vision that inspires you is overload. So if you have a goal or vision that inspires the hell out of you but also immediately overwhelms you, break it down into small goals and then into smaller, bite-sized steps.

While I didn't climb Mount Everest while travelling around Nepal, I did meet a few hardcore climbers who did. They explained to me about the series of base camps that are set up at increasing altitudes to give aspiring climbers the opportunity to acclimatise to the increasingly rare air before they continue on their upward ascent. Every expedition includes days for resting, recovering and acclimatising to ensure the climbers' maximum chance of success. Likewise, it's smart to break down your big vision into smaller, less daunting goals that are more doable in the short to medium term.

MAKE DAILY STROKES OF EFFORT

As you move forward in building momentum, be mindful that sometimes you may need to take a rest from your risk-taking, restock your reserves and reassess — which direction do you want to take next time you head out of your comfort zone? Don't make yourself wrong when you make a choice to play safe. Sometimes that's the best choice for you at that moment, given everything else going on in your life. Whatever choices you make or actions you take, just own them — along with the benefits and costs of making them.

William James, the father of modern psychology, prescribed that people make 'daily strokes of effort' towards their goals so they become more comfortable with the discomfort of stepping outside their comfort zone.

Breaking down your big goals and aspirations into more doable short-term goals and specific action tasks sets you up for success, when it comes to staying in action daily. These things may include more mundane actions — such as signing up for a course or brushing off your CV — but challenge yourself to do at least one thing daily that pushes you out of your comfort zone. It could be making a phone call you've been putting off; setting up a meeting with your boss to discuss promotion opportunities, or with a client prospect to pitch for new business; addressing a long-standing issue with someone; volunteering to lead a project team; attending a networking event; or introducing yourself to someone in your industry who can help your career.

> **The more you act with courage, the more courageous you'll become. Life rewards action. Always has. Always will.**

SET A VISION THAT COMPELS YOU TO BREAK RANKS WITH COMFORT

Scientists have found that the mental process of visualising completing any task fires the same neurons in the brain as if you were doing the actual task. When a tennis player visualises hitting the ball hurtling towards them at 200 kilometres per hour, they're activating the same sections of the brain as they would if they actually did hit the ball. Visualisation creates an internal comfort zone so that when you're in the real-life situation, the actions you need to take are more familiar. You've essentially taken them already, reducing your anxiety and improving your performance.

The power of visualisation can be applied just as much to a sales presentation, a difficult conversation with a colleague or a job interview or a long-held goal.

Imagine yourself succeeding in whatever situation you aspire to do well in, whether it's giving a knock-out sales presentation, running a business, or managing a large team of people. Picture yourself in a specific situation, feeling confident and able to respond comfortably to whatever happens with the sense of self-assurance, humour and focus needed to achieve whatever it is you want. Imagine yourself in the role you'd really like to have — capable, purposeful and ready to make whatever changes are required to produce the outcome you want. When you imagine this, visualise yourself being the most courageous version of who you are. This sets the stage for you to engage in any conversation, handle any situation and take on any challenge with the confidence needed to make it a success.

Just as we are all inspired by a different vision, everyone has their own path to forge and their own brand of bravery to build. Like the lion in *The Wizard of Oz*, too often we undermine our own courage by falling into the trap of thinking we should possess the same courage we see in others. Not so. Don't fail to exercise your own courage because you're preoccupied with making negative and disempowering comparisons with others. The way I see it, if we were all supposed to be like Bear Grylls, God would have made us all that way. The advice that Glinda the Good Witch gave to Dorothy in Oz applies just as much to you: *You've always had the power right there in your shoes; you just had to learn it for yourself.*

MAKE YOUR STAND FOR GREATNESS

It's a well-worn saying that if you don't stand for something, you'll fall for anything. In today's fearful and uncertain world, that usually means succumbing to the temptation to take the path of least resistance and greatest safety. If you picked up this book because the title spoke to you, then it's possible you've already journeyed down that path, at least in some way, and you know that it won't take you towards any destination you're inspired to travel to.

This book began by inviting you to ponder the question 'For the sake of what?' as it related to how you'll use your time, energy and talents over the course of your working life. Knowing what you want your life to stand for is an irreplaceable prerequisite for courage. So as you get ready to start taking actions you may never have taken before, ones that take you outside your comfort zone in different ways and new directions, it's vital to make a stand for greatness. As you know so well, it's all too easy to find reasons not to take the actions you know would benefit you. Too busy. Too tired. Too uncertain. Too soon. Too late. Too much effort. Too little guarantee. But people who live extraordinary lives don't settle for ordinary excuses.

Making a stand for greatness means giving up living a life that's run by excuses, justifications and insecurity. Of course, in the short term it's often hard to find the motivation to make the extra effort — to go the extra mile. Effort takes work. Work can be … well, tiresome at least, loathsome at worst — in any case, for those who don't see any utility in it beyond its immediate, often financial, reward. That's why it's important to look at what you do through the lens of your entire life and to decide that you will make a stand for something, whether for your own innate potential or for something far beyond you. For your children or your children's children. Or for people you may never know but who matter to you anyway. So let me ask you a question:

What is so important that it's enough for you to go the extra mile, forgoing the ease and familiar safety of the status quo?

In *Man's Search for Meaning*, Viktor Frankl wrote of the specific vocation or mission we each have in our lives, stating that 'everyone's task is as unique as is his specific opportunity to implement it'.

Of course as soon as you put this book down you will be faced with choices that will put your commitment to courage to the test. Your innate bias to discount the cost of playing safe will quickly kick in and the voice of fear will grow loud. *What if you fail? What will people say? Who are you to do that anyway?*

When it does, talk back to it: What would courage do right now?

Sometimes the answer will be clear. Other times it won't. You'll have to weigh up the pros and cons, evaluate the risks, assess your ability to handle it before making your choice. No-one can do that for you. You alone have to decide and you alone have to live with the outcome. But remember, our psychological immune system can far more easily justify an excess of courage than an excess of cowardice.

EMBRACE YOUR FUTURE AS THE ONCE IN A LIFETIME ADVENTURE IT IS

As I finish this now, still relatively 'fresh off the boat' from landing back in the USA from Asia (December 2020 was definitely not the easiest time to have relocated to America), and with a blank canvas of possibilities ahead, I hope that you will join me in re-imagining a future that ignites something deep within you, and then taking a brave step towards it.

And then tomorrow, another.

And if you sometimes don't land the outcome you want, learn the lesson and move on. Nothing worthwhile has ever been achieved with a guarantee of success. Nothing ever will be.

ACKNOWLEDGEMENTS

Firstly, I want to thank the many brave-hearted leaders who have shared their insights with me, from corporate titans like Bill Marriott to trailblazing entrepreneurs like Richard Branson. It's been an absolute privilege to learn from your hard-won wisdom first-hand.

When I wrote the first edition of *Stop Playing Safe*, my four children were aged nine to 14. Life was busy, if not outright chaotic, and I'd unlikely have taken on writing this book — nor, for that fact, any of my books — without my husband Andrew's constant encouragement and hands-on help at home. So, Andrew, thank you for everything, but most of all for constantly encouraging me to back myself more, doubt myself less and shine my light as boldly as I can.

I also want to acknowledge my four brave-hearted and all-round awesome kids — Lachlan, Maddy, Ben and Matthew. As the deadline for completing the original manuscript of this book drew closer, you cut me slack many times, including for countless burnt dinners. While your paths are yet to be forged, you've already shown that you're not going to settle for less than the biggest life you are capable of living. Watching you spread your wings can be bittersweet at times, but it's also one of the greatest privileges of my life.

Heartfelt thanks also go to all the team at John Wiley & Sons, but particularly Lucy Raymond. I recall sitting in a cafe with Lucy in St Kilda, Melbourne, on a cold winter's day, talking about the book I wanted to write and imagining this one into being. Lucy, you've backed me all the way many times now. Thank you.

Finally, a shout-out to my extended Kleinitz family and dear friends — near and far, new and old. There are more names to list than space allows but you know who you are so I hope you know how much I value your friendship over the miles and years. Mum and Dad, you top that list — thank you for always telling me how proud you are of me. I'm so proud of you too.

With gratitude to all with whom I have shared my journey so far. The adventure continues.

margie

INDEX

facial expressions, simulating
44–45
Fairfax, Warwick, *Crucible
Leadership* 130
fear
—of awkward conversations
67–68
—knowing what to 34–36
—perceiving 34
—and risk 23–25, 31
fear-casting, taming 36–37
fear-casts 113
The Fearless Organization, Amy
Edmondson 137
feedback, daring to give 80–82
The Five Dysfunctions of a Team,
Patrick Lencioni 145
flexible plans (flexi-plans)
101–102
forecasting opportunities
106–107
forecasts
—turning into fear-casts 113
—wrong 95–96
Frank (author's brother) and
motorbike accident 128–130
Frankl, Viktor, *Man's Search for
Meaning* 6, 174
Friedman, Tom 106
From the Ground Up, Howard
Shultz 144
Fromm, Erich 98
Furstenberg *see* von Furstenberg
future
—embracing your 175–176
—inspiring vision of 151

Gardner, John W 9
Garfield, Charles, *Peak Performers*
157
Garver, Lori 78–79
Geus *see* de Geus
The Gift of Fear, Gavin
de Becker 35
Gilbert, Daniel
—and negative forecasting
bias 113
—*Stumbling on Happiness* 42
Goethe *see* von Goethe
going the extra mile 161
Golem effect 153
Goleman, Daniel, *Emotional
Intelligence* 155
Goodwin, Leo 96
Gottman, John, *Why Marriages
Succeed or Fail* 148
greatness, standing for 173–175

habits, creating 167–169
The Happiness Advantage, Shawn
Achor 144–145
hardiness 112
Harvard Business Review,
study in 85
horn, blowing your own 77–78
*How Winning Leaders Make Great
Calls*, Noel Tichy and Warren
Bennis 157

inaction, cost of cautious 38–40
innate strengths 16–17
integrity 49–53
interviews, nervousness in 43

WE ARE BRAVER TOGETHER THAN ALONE

If the insights in these pages have helped you in any way, I'd love to stay connected and support you in navigating the risks ahead with greater clarity, confidence and courage.

SOCIAL MEDIA

I regularly post videos, articles and insights on my social channels. Please say hello!

FREE LIVE BRAVELY VIDEO COURSE

To help you apply the insights in this book to 'level up' in your career, leadership and life, subscribe to my four part Live Bravely video series (with a 'no spam' promise!). Details at **www.margiewarrell.com/livebravely**

KEYNOTE SPEAKING

Empowering audiences at conferences and events is something that lights me up. If you're looking for a dynamic speaker to ignite a spark in people attending your event, I'd love to hear from you. Watch videos and learn more at **www.margiewarrell.com/speaking**

KORN FERRY CEO & LEADERSHIP ADVISORY

Korn Ferry leads the world in unlocking the potential in people and organisations. As a key member of their CEO Succession & Leadership Development practice my team would love to support your organisation in unlocking the talent in your team. Learn more and connect via **www.KornFerry.com**

MEDIA & INTERVIEWS

Media enquiries can be made via **www.margiewarrell.com/media**

THE LIVE BRAVE PODCAST

Listen to my insights and the wisdom of other big thinkers, luminaries and leaders — including many whose insights have been included in this book — on my Live Brave Podcast. Listen on Apple podcasts, Spotify or online at **www.thelivebravepodcast.com**

KEEP READING

If you enjoyed this book, check out Margie's other books which include the titles below.

YOU'VE GOT THIS!

A masterclass to build self-trust, beat self-doubt and make you boldest aspirations a reality.

Filled with heart and humour but grounded in research, this handbook will help unleash your untapped potential and passion, creativity and courage, to thrive in today's uncertain world. A must read for anyone who needs encouragement to rise and take that leap.

TRAIN THE BRAVE

Fifty uplifting chapters with practical strategies to build your bravery and thrive in work, love and life.

Originally published as Brave (Wiley, 2015), this book is for busy people looking for a regular shot of inspiration. The 50 easy-to-read chapters will inspire you to 'train the brave' in every area of your life.

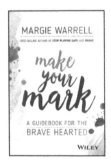

MAKE YOUR MARK

A guidebook to get unstuck and on track to your biggest life.

Your 7-step roadmap to help you make the changes you've been putting off and get 'on purpose' to make your unique mark with greater clarity, confidence and courage. To be read with a pen in hand!